Transforming the Curriculum

Preparing Students for a Changing World

Elizabeth A. Jones

ASHE-ERIC Higher Education Report: Volume 29, Number 3
Adrianna J. Kezar, Series Editor

Prepared and published by

JOSSEY-BASS
A Wiley Imprint
www.josseybass.com

In cooperation with

ERIC Clearinghouse on Higher Education
The George Washington University
URL: www.eriche.org

Association for the Study
of Higher Education
URL: www.tiger.coe.missouri.edu/~ashe

Graduate School of Education and Human Development
The George Washington University
URL: www.gwu.edu

Transforming the Curriculum: Preparing Students for a Changing World
Elizabeth A. Jones
ASHE-ERIC Higher Education Report: Volume 29, Number 3
Adrianna J. Kezar, Series Editor

This publication was prepared partially with funding from the Office of Educational Research and Improvement, U.S. Department of Education, under contract no. ED-99-00-0036. The opinions expressed in this report do not necessarily reflect the positions or policies of OERI or the Department.

ISSN 0884-0040   electronic ISSN 1536-0709   ISBN 0-7879-6348-8

The ASHE-ERIC Higher Education Report is part of the Jossey-Bass Higher and Adult Education Series and is published six times a year by Wiley Subscription Services, Inc., A Wiley Company, at Jossey-Bass, 989 Market Street, San Francisco, California 94103-1741.

For subscription information, see the Back Issue/Subscription Order Form in the back of this journal.

CALL FOR PROPOSALS: Prospective authors are strongly encouraged to contact Adrianna Kezar at (301) 405-0868 or kezar@wam.umd.edu.

Visit the Jossey-Bass Web site at **www.josseybass.com.**

Printed in the United States of America on acid-free recycled paper.

Executive Summary

Many faculty, employers, and policymakers agree that college students should be skilled communicators and problem solvers (Jones, 1996). The quantity and complexity of information have increased dramatically and can be overwhelming for new professionals who must learn to gather, organize, and manage it. College graduates are encountering new problems in changing contexts.

Ideally, an undergraduate education should provide students with the necessary critical skills, attitudes, and values to successfully navigate the dynamic complexities of the business world. Employers are searching for graduates with strong abilities in problem solving, teamwork, communications, and leadership (Carnevale, 2000; Rao and Sylvester, 2000; Oblinger and Verville, 1998; Miles, 1994). Although most employees enter new positions with adequate technical skills, it is the process skills (especially communications and problem solving) that count toward successful job performance over time, and it is these skills that are most often absent (College Placement Council, 1994).

Concerns about the educational quality of professional preparation programs have generated fairly specific sets of recommendations about the interventions or reforms necessary to strengthen undergraduate education. Some reports are very critical, while others suggest that the gap exists today between the ideal outcomes and actual performance because there has been considerable "upskilling" across sectors of different professional fields (Business–Higher Education Forum, 1997; Carnevale, Gainer, and Meltzer, 1990).

Very little recent information regarding the progress that has been made in the United States has been synthesized and analyzed in response to these criticisms. The majority of this report focuses on the major changes that college and university faculty have designed in their undergraduate professional education programs in accounting, nursing, and teacher education. Each area represents a different emphasis. Accounting is characterized as an enterprising field, nursing as a helping profession, and education as an informing profession (Stark, Lowther, and Hagerty, 1986). Examples of curriculum reforms in each of these professional preparation areas are highlighted. They represent comprehensive changes across the academic program that are designed to enhance students' communications (oral and written), problem-solving or critical thinking abilities and related dispositions, information competencies, or teamwork and collaboration. For each example, the learning outcomes that faculty want students to achieve, the structure of the revised curriculum and learning experiences, and highlights of assessment results are discussed. The challenges faced by faculty teams profiled in this report and their curriculum changes are not unique to their fields. These changes offer insightful lessons for faculty in many different disciplines, especially those who work with students in various professional fields.

It is evident from a review of these curriculum reforms that the learning-centered paradigm is being embraced by some groups of faculty as they create and implement major curriculum reforms. Collectively, such reforms require students to be actively engaged in their studies. Faculty design the curriculum with an emphasis on getting students to work on real-world issues or problems, often in teams. These problems are usually open-ended, with no single right answer. Ambiguous features often require students to reflect on real-life factors as they make reasoned judgments. Professors become coaches or guides who facilitate learning rather than solely monitor it. More authentic assessments of student learning are used to gauge whether students are mastering the intended learning outcomes.

The examples of curriculum reform serve as highlights of significant changes rather than a comprehensive portrait of all efforts. Some faculty and administrators have initiated and implemented major curriculum changes, expecting to strengthen student learning by placing a particular emphasis on improving critical thinking, communications skills, or information literacy.

An important feature of many professional preparation programs is a strong internship experience. Faculty extend internships for longer periods of time and across the curriculum rather than waiting until the senior year. In addition, internships are being linked to foster stronger connections with learning outcomes, such as problem solving and working in teams. Through these experiences, students get the opportunity to test their abilities to transfer what they have learned to actual work contexts and get feedback from multiple assessors that is targeted to help them improve.

The reform processes discussed in this report emphasize that serious initiatives require a systematic approach across the curriculum rather than selective interventions by an individual faculty member in a single course. Isolated changes are less likely to have a major impact on student learning. Such major changes are not easy for faculty to consider and adopt without serious attention to several key aspects that help build a culture open to change. This report concludes with a set of recommendations and critical elements that must be addressed for change to occur and be sustained over long periods of time. The curriculum reform process is dynamic and continuous, and faculty leaders need to create trust and demonstrate their real commitments through guiding planned change that has incentives for faculty to participate. In addition, an open process includes faculty in the reform process from the very beginning through implementation and evaluation. In successful reform initiatives, teams of faculty leaders have thoughtfully planned and developed a series of ongoing faculty development activities. Faculty need ongoing learning opportunities to help create a new or revised curriculum. Finally, attention to the development of a strong assessment process is critical to determine the impact that a new program has on student learning and development. Strong assessments provide meaningful information that faculty can use to make informed decisions about changes that should be made to strengthen student learning.

Contents

Foreword

Since the mid-1980s, higher education leaders have been in a protracted process of reexamining the curriculum. Critics and policymakers through national reports such as *Investment in Learning* question pedagogical techniques, curricular coherence, lack of focus on student outcomes, and the separation of in- and out-of-classroom learning. General education, in particular, has received a great deal of scrutiny the last two decades. Hundreds if not thousands of institutions across the country have revised their general education requirements. In the 1990s, reforms continued to mount in higher education, but more attention was focused on teaching, faculty roles, and new challenges such as technology. Although there have been a plethora of discussions related to general education reform, professional education has received less attention. Elizabeth Jones fills this gap in the literature with her monograph *Preparing Students for a Changing World*. The curricular reform of professional education includes efforts to address some of the criticisms lodged against general education (such as a greater focus on student outcomes), yet many areas are unique—responding to new professional standards, defining competencies, and requirements for internships, for example. Jones, associate professor at West Virginia University, has spent several years conducting research in the area of professional education, establishing a record as an expert in this changing field. In this monograph, she follows up on the important work of individuals such as Hoberman and groups such as the American Council on Education's Business–Higher Education Forum report on the expectations of employers. After describing the calls for reform, she reviews a host of the most significant curricular outcomes and innovations. Some of the major ideas she presents are the need for new skills among professionals such as leadership or systems thinking, performance in cross-functional teams, technology, and an appreciation for diversity. Her focus is on documenting changes that institutions have made to respond to calls for reform. She hones in on a few key professional areas—accounting, nursing, and teacher education—to provide depth to the many complex changes. Case examples of particular institutions and cross-institutional projects provide the reader with key data for creating these reforms on their own campus. Jones also highlights areas where minimal progress has been made, enabling leaders to see where more curricular reform is needed.

Having ideas for change is usually not enough to actually implement the reforms. Jones anticipates this issue and provides leaders with plans for helping faculty consider adoption of curricular changes. No book is as comprehensive in scope in reviewing professional education reforms. Perhaps the most exciting aspect of this monograph is that it highlights programs where faculty have created student-centered learning plans and where a broad range of competencies are being developed that meet the challenges of an increasingly altered work environment. Curriculum revisions will most likely become a process that faculty will have to engage in on a more ongoing basis than in the past. Thus, understanding ways to encourage this process is essential for an administrator or leader in higher education. I applaud Beth Jones for building a framework to guide not only professional education reform but also curriculum reform in general.

Several other ASHE-ERIC monographs may also interest readers: Brookhart's *The Art and Science of Assessment,* which describes the major tenets of Jones's framework for curricular revisions in even more depth; Maitland and Shilling's *Proclaiming and Sustaining Excellence: Assessment as a Faculty Role;* and Weidman, Twale, and Stein's excellent overview of graduate education, *Socialization of Graduate and Professional Students in Higher Education.*

Adrianna J. Kezar
ASHE-ERIC Series Editor
University of Maryland

Acknowledgments

I greatly appreciate the support that I received from my family, especially my father, mother, and sister. We have faced some challenging times, and their consistent support helped this report to be completed. I also thank the late Dr. Donald Farmer, the academic vice president at King's College and a visionary whom I greatly admired. He particularly influenced my thoughts and ideas expressed in the last section of this report. Dr. Farmer openly shared with me his innovative leadership ideas during this past decade. Finally, I appreciate the insights of the anonymous reviewers who suggested ways to strengthen this work. Their feedback was meaningful and their suggested revisions incorporated when possible.

Introduction

MANY FACULTY, EMPLOYERS, and policymakers agree that college students should be skilled communicators and problem solvers (Jones, 1996). The quantity and complexity of information have increased dramatically and can be overwhelming for new professionals who must learn to gather, organize, and manage it. In addition, many unpredictable changes are unfolding as a result of technological developments and the globalization of business environments. With this increased complexity and uncertainty, college graduates are encountering new problems in changing contexts.

Ideally, an undergraduate education should provide students with the necessary skills, abilities, attitudes, and values that are critical to successfully navigate the dynamic complexities of the business world. In these business environments, new college graduates encounter a demanding and highly competitive job market characterized by major transformations in an increasingly diverse environment.

> New college graduates encounter a demanding and highly competitive job market characterized by major transformations in an increasingly diverse environment.

Specialized technical knowledge has always been particularly important for undergraduates majoring in professional preparation programs. But increasingly, employers are searching for employees who have strong abilities in such areas as problem solving, teamwork, communications, leadership, learning, and systems thinking (Carnevale, 2000; Rao and Sylvester, 2000; Oblinger and Verville, 1998; Miles, 1994).

Although most employees enter new positions with adequate technical skills, it is the general skills (especially communications and problem solving) that count toward successful job performance over time, and it is these skills that are most absent (College Placement Council, 1994). In addition, college students view these skills as crucial and necessary to ensure their own career mobility (Education Commission of the States, 1995).

The Changing Business Environment and the Need for Responsive Action

Today business corporations are dramatically changing the way they conduct their daily routines. Although many changes are occurring simultaneously, a few major trends will be presented that have a great impact on business environments. Ultimately, these changes have significant implications for the reform of professional education programs.

The use of cross-functional, multidisciplinary teams with globally and ethnically diverse memberships is growing rapidly (Boyett and Snyder, 1998). Already, one-third of American companies with fifty or more employees have half or more of their employees working in self-managed or problem-solving teams (Boyett and Snyder, 1998). Many of these teams have no formal boss or supervisor; rather, the team members take on responsibilities for planning, organizing, staffing, scheduling, directing, monitoring, and controlling their own work. They more frequently identify problems and make crucial decisions that were formerly made by their managers. These teams are increasingly linked through Internet or other global networks, with instantaneous and unrestricted flows of information within and between teams and team members and among external stakeholders, including customers. Charles Manz and Henry Sims (1993), based on their research studies, believe that nearly every major company in the United States is trying or considering some form of empowered work teams in parts of their organizations. They estimate that in the new millennium "approximately 40 to 50 percent of the entire workforce in the United States will work in some type of empowered, self-managed team" (p. 12). The major benefits of these teams are "increased productivity, improved quality, enhanced employee quality of work life, reduced costs, reduced turnover and absenteeism, reduced conflict, increased innovation and better organizational adaptability and flexibility" (p. 8).

As companies flatten their organizational hierarchies, another major feature of these new structures is increased job responsibilities (Useem, 1995). For example, managers at lower levels are expected to oversee several functions rather than specializing in finance, engineering, marketing, research, or sales. Now they need to fully understand all these major functions. In addition, the roles of managers have changed from supervising or directing to teaching, building consensus, and empowering and supporting employees (Marshall, 2000). Furthermore, company managers and leaders are listening more to their diverse customers and colleagues (Useem, 1995).

Another major force in the external environment is the accelerating rate of change and complexity in technology. The rapid expansion and influx of interactive telecommunications networks linking individuals and organizations to extensive data resources through workstations and computers capable of integrating information, sound, and video images are creating unprecedented opportunities (Peterson and Dill, 1997). Several critical aspects are associated in this computer revolution that dramatically impact on all organizations: (1) its rapid development and rate of change; (2) the extent to which applications are being adopted in many areas of the workplace; (3) its spread to both national and international arenas in a short time; (4) its potential for use with few constraints of time and location; and (5) the increased affordability of increasingly stronger technologies (Peterson and Dill, 1997).

Advances in technology strengthen the capacity of various organizations to reach and interact with colleagues and customers in new ways. "Rapid technological development adds layers of ethical complexity to the decisions made by individuals" (Commission on Admission to Graduate Management Education, 1990, p. 5). As the boundaries of new technology expand, the number of ethical decisions made by employees also increase. Both new, expanded knowledge of technology and new skills in conceptualizing and rapidly solving unprecedented problems have become essential (Commission on Admission to Graduate Management Education, 1990).

The dramatic changes in technology have created a more global economic system. This globalization of business creates a stronger need for undergraduates to understand different cultures and their own values, beliefs, and behaviors. However, "the curricula of business schools have recently concentrated far more on the building of elegant, abstract models that seek to unify the world economic system than on the development of frameworks to help students understand the messy, concrete reality of international business" (Commission on Admission to Graduate Management Education, 1990, p. 7). Dexterity in working across boundaries and learning from others is a valuable asset to many corporations (Useem, 1995).

The changing demographics of the workforce have a major impact on various markets. This new diversity includes changes in age, gender, racial and ethnic backgrounds, and national origins to the workforce that graduates of business schools will manage (Commission on Admission to Graduate Management Education, 1990). The numbers of almost all minority groups are increasing and will continue into the future (Peterson and Dill, 1997). For example, the ethnic group growing in largest proportion is individuals of Hispanic origin. After 1996, the Hispanic population is projected to add more persons to the United States population every year than any other race or ethnic group (Fink, 1997). In 1993, the United States population of Hispanic origin totaled twenty-five million; it is projected to nearly triple to eighty-eight million individuals in 2050 (Fink, 1997). Such changes in ethnic composition will occur at very different rates in different states, with California experiencing the highest levels of diversity. By 2040, it is projected that California's population will be one-third white, with approximately one-half of the state's population being of Hispanic origin (Fink, 1997).

All these major changes in business environments have great implications for the revision and reform of the professional education curriculum. Michael Useem (1995, p. 23) astutely questions whether students "will . . . be prepared to acquire knowledge later in a work environment that stresses personal initiative and collaborative work" if they "acquire knowledge by passively listening to authoritative figures at the lectern and experience no dialogue with them or with themselves." College graduates will be working in dynamic environments where they will be expected to work in teams to solve complex problems with numerous alternatives. College graduates will need to examine and judge different options and then select the best alternative. They will be expected to make informed decisions often in very ambiguous conditions. The ability to learn will be extremely important as new graduates manipulate and work with abstract symbols, simulations, and models. The sharing of information and cooperative efforts to achieve common objectives will be crucial for business organizations as they implement high-quality processes (Marshall, 2000). Professional education programs will need to reexamine their overall curriculum, including the important outcomes that all college graduates should master to be more effective in the changing workplace.

Defining Professional Education and Ideal Outcomes

Given the enormous body of literature pertaining to professional education, this report will focus on baccalaureate degree programs. Although certification and continuing education are important, these topics are beyond the scope of this current review. Professional preparation programs typically involve three different emphases: (1) helping (such as nursing or social work); (2) enterprising (such as business or engineering); and (3) informing (such as education or journalism) (Stark, Lowther, and Hagerty, 1986). Across these different emphases, there are common expectations about the key competencies and attitudes that college graduates need to be successful in the workplace. Competent professionals are frequently characterized by their abilities to link technical knowledge with appropriate values and attitudes when making complex judgments within ambiguous contexts (Stark and Lowther, 1988). Four sets of competencies across professional fields have been identified by Stark and Lowther:

- *Conceptual competence:* Understanding the theoretical foundations of the profession;
- *Technical competence:* Ability to perform skills required by the profession;
- *Integrative competence:* Ability to meld theory and skills in the practice setting; and
- *Career marketability:* Becoming marketable as a result of acquired education and training. [1988, p. 21]

Strong professional education programs usually supplement conceptual competence with concerns about the integration of important liberal learning outcomes (Stark and Lowther, 1988). Such specific outcomes frequently include communication competencies. College graduates are expected to read, write, speak, and listen effectively to develop and convey ideas, solutions or alternatives, and information (Jones, 1996). In addition, college graduates are expected to solve complex problems and identify numerous alternatives before selecting the best option (Jones, 1996). As students work on these open-ended problems, they also can develop certain dispositions such as being open-minded and flexible. Increasingly, college graduates are expected to work in teams and collaborate with each other as they strive to solve complex problems (Jones, 1996). Finally, leadership and ethics are important as college graduates adapt to changing environments and make important decisions (Stark and Lowther, 1988).

Carnevale, Gainer, and Meltzer (1990) also studied the important competencies associated with professional education necessary to succeed in the workplace. They discovered seven broad sets of skills that are essential to foster effective learning on the job for new employees. The basic skills listed below are important for most employees, not just white-collar and technical professionals, such as engineers.

- *Learning to learn:* Ability to distinguish between essential and nonessential information, discern patterns in information, and pinpoint the actions necessary to improve performance;
- *Reading, writing, and computation:* Ability to understand and communicate information through high-quality documents and to perform mathematical calculations;
- *Oral communication and listening:* Ability to speak effectively in public and to communicate with others;
- *Creative thinking and problem solving:* Ability to identify and define problems, create and implement innovative solutions, and track and evaluate results;
- *Personal management:* Ability to have strong self-esteem and high motivation through setting goals and to enhance career development skills to understand and plan for professional paths beyond entry-level employment;

- *Group effectiveness:* Ability to develop strong interpersonal skills necessary to work effectively in teams and develop negotiation skills; and
- *Organizational effectiveness and leadership:* Ability to understand "how the organization works and how the actions of each individual affect organizational and strategic objectives" (p. 34). Leadership is "achieved by cultivating the respect of peers and projecting a sense of reliability, goal orientation, and vision" (p. 34).

Certain specific educational outcomes are important for college graduates to master to be effective in the workplace. These research studies provide insights about the nature of the ideal levels of outcomes that new employees should possess to fully perform in their new professional roles.

Examining Criticisms of Professional Education and Calls for Reform

Professionals in diverse fields readily recognize the major changes in the business environment. Frequently, these changes have prompted faculty, administrators, employers, and policymakers to respond with formal reports calling for substantive changes in professional education programs. Hundreds of reports and articles critique the preparation of professionals. Some articles represent the beliefs of an individual and are often portrayed in the media as anecdotal comments criticizing the preparation of professionals. Very few analytical research studies have closely examined this issue. However, employers, undergraduates, and college alumni do have perspectives about their own preparation for the workplace. This section presents a brief overview of the main common themes across the literature.

Employer Beliefs About College Graduates' Preparation for the Workplace

Criticisms about professional education have been major issues reiterated over time. Debates about the content of the education and the actual preparation of undergraduates to be effective practitioners have been serious points contested by different groups. Employers want a new kind of professional with a broad set of workplace skills and a strong foundation in the basics that will facilitate his or her learning in new positions. More than a decade ago, the Commission on Workforce Quality and Labor Market Efficiency (1989) asserted that employers increasingly report difficulty in finding the new employees they need. More recently, Van Horn (1995), in a formal study of New Jersey employers, found that business supervisors believed that at most one-third of their recent college graduates were "highly prepared for work." In addition, corporate leaders across the United States agreed that college graduates were weak in a number of key areas, including "leadership and communication skills; quantification skills; interpersonal relations; the ability to work in teams; the understanding to work with a diverse work force at home and abroad; and the capacity to adapt to rapid change" (Business–Higher Education Forum, 1995, p. 3). Similar results were found in 1997 when the Business–Higher Education Forum conducted interviews with employers and college alumni. Respondents continued to emphasize weaknesses in "the ability to communicate orally and in writing, interpersonal and leadership skills, the capacity to contribute to and participate in teams, analytical ability, and adaptability" (Business–Higher Education Forum, 1997, p. 20). These results correlate with the findings from a large mail survey conducted by the National Association of Colleges and Universities (1995). Deficiencies in many of these types of skills are barriers to entry-level, experienced employees, and to dislocated workers attempting to adapt to economic and technological change in diverse companies (Carnevale, Gainer, and Meltzer, 1990).

In a national study, Jones (1997) found that employers believed college graduates frequently lacked the ability to solve complex, ill-structured problems. Employers were particularly troubled that the new college graduates they employed had great difficulty identifying multiple solutions for problems. Employees often searched for the single "right" answer and seldom offered alternatives, even when they were asked to develop multiple strategies. Collectively, these reports wanted higher education institutions to prepare more competent professionals who can deliver or provide effective quality services.

Although some reports calling for reform are based on larger studies or feedback from business leaders across the United States, other studies frequently are based on research conducted at one particular institution. For example, employers who hired college graduates from a research university were asked to evaluate the quality of business school graduates. Employers indicated that they were most satisfied with graduates' professional attitudes and their technical abilities (Paranto and Champagne, 1996). However, employers reported their lowest level of satisfaction with written communication skills and the weak abilities to apply knowledge to real-world situations. Collectively, these types of reports demonstrate a dramatic challenge of the academy's traditional belief that mastery of the discipline should be the principal measure of collegiate success (Ewell, 1997).

Current Student and Alumni Views About Their Preparation for the Workplace

Some individual institutions survey alumni of their baccalaureate programs. However, these types of studies are usually based in one particular university and do not provide a comprehensive picture of strengths and weaknesses associated with college graduates' preparation for the workforce. Therefore, it is difficult to actually know the real performance of new graduates in diverse settings in the workplace and whether they are in reality fully prepared for their new roles. A review of a sample of single institution–based studies reveals some common concerns, however.

Gardner and Motschenbacher (1993) asked recent technical college graduates (engineers and computer scientists) to identify the skills where they believed they were best prepared. Graduates reported that their strengths were mainly the specific technical skills that they learned for their specific majors and the specific problem-solving processes emphasized by their own faculty. These college graduates believed that they were weakest in their written and oral communication skills. They reported struggling to work in teams and viewed their leadership and management skills as being deficient. In particular, engineers were concerned about their abilities to apply theoretical knowledge to real work contexts.

An exploratory study at Michigan State University continues to support these types of findings. Gardner (1998) investigated the workplace readiness of college students by placing undergraduates in a simulation similar to a task required for the workplace. Students demonstrated that they "know how pieces of information are interrelated but did not do as well in assessing the accuracy of their information by using other references, or in evaluating the usefulness of information in the context being applied" (p. 71). Students frequently chose an appropriate strategy to achieve the organizational goals, but they often neglected to consider a diverse range of options that limited the alternatives available to them. In this study, students demonstrated weaker performances in their interpersonal skills, particularly working in teams. Students "were frustrated in trying to identify options that reduced conflict among team members and often failed to work in a manner that contributed to the unity and success of the team" (pp. 71–72). They also lacked the ability to persuade or convince others to support their position through a presentation or discussion (Gardner, 1998).

Alumni were directly asked to provide feedback about the quality of the civil engineering program at Virginia Polytechnic Institute and State University. These alumni served on an advisory board and critiqued this particular undergraduate professional program during a formal dinner and then through a survey distributed to nine members of the board. The results indicated that the alumni believed that students were strongly prepared technically and very computer literate (Walker and Muffo, 1996). However, students needed better preparation to communicate and work in teams, according to the alumni. Additional research at this same institution found that undergraduates had very traditional views about the importance of communication skills. They believed writing topics (such as sentence structure, grammar, punctuation, and spelling) to be important considerations only for English composition classes (Muffo and Metz, 1996). Students did not believe that the correct use of language should be examined when they write in courses for their particular major. This study demonstrates the challenge in working with students and trying to help them understand the importance of strong communication abilities, especially in relation to different contexts, including preparation for the workplace. Faculty (at Virginia Polytechnic Institute and State University) thought that students would take writing more seriously if it were emphasized in major courses. In addition, faculty believed that employers place a strong emphasis on written communication skills and that multiple writing opportunities across courses could help students synthesize ideas better.

Therefore, faculty are exploring ways to integrate writing across different courses required for various majors.

A consistent theme emerges across the different sources of data and information about employer and alumni perceptions of their own preparation for the workplace. College graduates are generally well prepared for the technical competencies associated with their new jobs. For example, a new accountant fully understands the relevant auditing procedures required for a particular position. But these new college graduates often lack the abilities to successfully communicate with diverse audiences and face difficulties working on teams to solve complex and open-ended problems. The transition from student life to the corporate sector is a particular challenge for new professionals, and the inability of college graduates to successfully manage the expectations of the workplace may in part be responsible for the high number of turnovers in the first eighteen months of employment (Holton, 1992; Louis, 1980).

The transition from student life to the corporate sector is a particular challenge for new professionals.

Recommendations for Change in Professional Education Programs

Although diverse stakeholders in higher education stress the importance of certain outcomes, many reports outline the challenges facing higher education in trying to reach these ideal goals. In fact, contemporary reports continue to emphasize and call for major reforms in the preparation of professionals who will enter the workforce in the future. A significant gap exists between the ideal professional education outcomes that are deemed necessary for effective performance in the workplace and the actual abilities and skill levels perceived by employers, supervisors, and recent college graduates. Concerns about the educational quality of professional preparation programs have generated fairly specific sets of recommendations about the interventions or reforms necessary to strengthen undergraduate education. Some reports are very critical, while others suggest that the gap exists increasingly today between the ideal outcomes and actual performance because there has been considerable "upskilling" across sectors of different professional fields (Business–Higher

Education Forum, 1997; Carnevale, Gainer, and Meltzer, 1990). The expectations for effective performance are much higher today than in previous decades because of major changes in business environments. Therefore, some reports conclude that college graduates are not well qualified to perform their positions in the current dramatically changing conditions in the workplace (Business–Higher Education Forum, 1997).

Specific recommendations include the following points:

- Establish ways to bring together faculty and corporate leaders so that faculty can learn about businesses' needs and business leaders can see what faculty members already do to prepare students for the work force;
- Identify cooperative practices involving business and higher education that have successfully influenced work-force preparation, and model future program on successful examples; and
- Explicitly define the skills and knowledge desired in new employees and analyze the learning experiences that facilitate these characteristics;
- Evaluate efforts to improve worker preparation by asking recently hired alumni how effective they believe their preparation to have been;
- Establish more developmental work opportunities and work simulations for students during their undergraduate education. [Business–Higher Education Forum, 1997, pp. 9–10]

In 1999, the Business–Higher Education Forum expanded on its sets of recommendations and suggested key responses that would help ensure that students acquire the skills and attributes essential to succeed in the workplace. Their suggestions included:

- The core curriculum needs to help students develop flexible and cross-functional skill sets, including leadership, teamwork, problem solving, time management, communication, and analytical thinking;

- Methods of helping students acquire or reinforce required personal traits, including ethics, adaptability, self-management, global consciousness, and a passion for life-long learning must be integrated into the core curriculum;
- Developing a collaborative process for restructuring curricula and teaching methods to keep pace with the constantly changing needs of today's global economy must become a critical priority for business and higher education;
- The academic sectors must provide more opportunities for college students to take theoretical concepts and apply them to "real" learning experiences;
- The academic-corporate dialogue should include faculty and focus on practical, action-oriented items to insure that college graduates are prepared for today's high-performance work place. [Business–Higher Education Forum, 1997, pp. 8–9]

These recommendations were developed to help particularly the academic sectors consider specific ways in which faculty and administrators could work to change the professional education curricula so that students would ideally become better prepared for the realities of the business environments.

From a comprehensive study of professional programs, Hoberman (1994) concludes that undergraduates should acquire research skills to become stronger practitioners who can learn from their own practice. He also encourages professional programs to move away from numerous specializations that can enrich offerings but also frequently lead to modular approaches. Such fragmentation from too much specialization often means that "relationships with other people, clients, support staff, colleagues, and persons in the service network tend to be ignored" (p. 184). Professional education should include an integrative sequence to help students see the full portrait of the profession's services. Another important recommendation is that natural experiential learning should be increased and improved. Hoberman (1994) suggests that through experiential learning, undergraduates can transfer their learning to new contexts, continue to learn from diverse experiences, learn to relate better with others, and cope with unanticipated events. Such experiences give undergraduates opportunities to link theory with practice, get frequent feedback, and reflect on and analyze their own progress.

Purpose and Scope of This Report

This introductory chapter contains a brief overview of the key criticisms and recommendations outlined in a sample of reports pertaining to professional programs in undergraduate education. Although these individual reports portray the weaknesses in college students' learning and development, there has been very little recent synthesis and analysis regarding *the progress* that has been made (in the United States) in response to these criticisms. The majority of this report focuses on the major changes that college and university faculty have designed in their undergraduate professional education programs to address specific concerns. Numerous examples across institutional contexts clearly demonstrate that some faculty have implemented major reforms in their professional education programs. The majority of attention is focused on reforms where some evidence exists of an impact on students' learning and development. Formal assessments of these curricular or programmatic reforms should demonstrate some type of effect on student learning.

The second chapter focuses specifically on innovations in the professional education curriculum designed to strengthen communication (oral or written), problem-solving, or critical thinking abilities and related dispositions, and teamwork and collaboration. These outcomes were selected because they are important across many professions, yet employers and recent alumni often report they have weak skills in these particular areas. Some innovations integrate several of these outcomes rather than addressing discrete or isolated skills, and they are sometimes linked with information literacy competencies. The third chapter examines how faculty and administrators can build stronger partnerships with employers through reforming their internship, fieldwork, and practicum experiences for undergraduates majoring in professional fields. The final chapter presents recommendations for encouraging faculty to seriously consider curricular reforms that are responsive to enhancing certain student outcomes. Concrete suggestions are provided to help faculty and administrators create, design, and implement curriculum innovations that are responsive to the needs of the workplace.

The synthesis and analysis of the relevant curricular innovations and their impact on student learning should be useful to several audiences. First, college and university administrators frequently search for good models to examine their features, design, and impact on student learning. Such a review of models can provide them with a stronger understanding of potential innovations that could be implemented and have direct applications for their own programs. Such models may be tailored to meet the needs of particular groups of students. Second, faculty in professional preparation programs and liberal arts may seek to strengthen their collaborations or partnerships with the intention of creating stronger learning experiences for undergraduates that help them to be more fully prepared for the workplace. Third, researchers and graduate students who study professional education may find this book useful as they seek to gather evidence about the quality of learning experiences developed for future professionals. Finally, professional accrediting associations and other policymakers may benefit from the synthesis and analysis presented in this report, especially as they seek ways to encourage colleges and universities to prepare stronger professionals to meet the demands in dynamic business environments.

Curriculum Reforms in the Professions: Responding to Calls for Change

FOR MANY YEARS, curriculum reform emphasized the teaching-centered paradigm in which faculty were considered the authorities who knew all the right answers (Huba and Freed, 2000; Barr and Tagg, 1995). In this paradigm, students passively received information and acquired knowledge that did not connect with contexts where it would be used (Huba and Freed, 2000; Barr and Tagg, 1995). Faculty often searched for new information, integrated it with existing knowledge, organized it for formal presentations to students, and explained it orally in class (Huba and Freed, 2000). Professors primarily presented current information in the discipline and then evaluated student learning to identify the appropriate grade to award. Students typically worked individually in a single discipline as they sought to satisfy their instructors. Assessment was mainly used to monitor student learning, with the major criterion being the articulation of right answers. Students were frequently assessed through objectively scored tests, including multiple-choice exams. The overall mission of colleges then was to provide instruction or deliver teaching by transferring knowledge from faculty to students. This teaching-centered paradigm led to piecemeal changes in the undergraduate curriculum. Few curriculum changes were adopted widely, and others often failed (Barr and Tagg, 1995).

Currently, some groups of faculty are embracing the learning-centered paradigm as they create and implement major curriculum reforms in their professional education programs. Collectively, such reforms require students to be actively involved. Typically, "students construct knowledge through gathering and synthesizing information and integrating it with the general skills of inquiry, communication, critical thinking, and problem solving" (Huba and Freed, 2000, p. 5). Faculty design the curriculum with an emphasis on getting students to work on real-world issues or problems, often in teams. These problems are usually open-ended and have no single right answer. Often, ambiguous features require students to reflect on real-life factors before making reasoned judgments. Professors become coaches or guides to facilitate learning rather than solely monitor it. Faculty and students work to create a culture that values and strives for collaboration. Assessment is used primarily to promote and diagnose learning (Huba and Freed, 2000). Faculty encourage students to generate insightful questions and learn from their mistakes rather than search for the sole right answer. Students often get opportunities to reflect on their performances or learning experiences. Frequent feedback from faculty and/or peers provides students with guidance about how to revise their work and substantially improve it. Therefore, assessments of student learning are frequently done through papers, projects, and portfolios. In this learning-centered paradigm, faculty focus on creating learning environments where the main purpose is to produce learning.

The major curriculum reforms explored in this monograph illustrate faculty who embrace the learning-centered paradigm and made extensive changes in their undergraduate professional preparation programs. Examples of major curriculum reforms discussed serve as highlights of significant changes rather than a comprehensive portrait of all efforts. Some faculty and administrators have initiated and implemented major curriculum changes with the expectation of strengthening student learning by placing a particular emphasis on certain skills, such as improving their critical thinking, problem-solving, or communication skills.

A special focus is placed on those professional preparation programs in the United States where groups of faculty are making changes across their curriculum. The primary attention in this chapter is on curriculum reforms where teams of faculty have intentionally decided to create and redesign a series of courses or entire professional education programs with the expectation of promoting stronger student learning. When groups of faculty implement change, the likelihood is greater that they will have more impact on student learning, as certain outcomes are emphasized and reinforced across multiple courses and sections. For this reason, a professor who has changed his or her own course is not the focus of this report. A professor may experiment with a new instructional strategy and then report his or her results. Although the work of an individual professor is important, the main criterion employed in selecting professional programs to profile in this report is groups of faculty who worked together to create major changes in their professional preparation programs. These faculty are articulating new student learning objectives or outcomes, changing the content and structure of their program, integrating new ways to work with students, and assessing learning outcomes to determine whether these changes have any impact on student learning and development. Each example profiled in this report varies in the depth that faculty provide about certain curriculum dimensions. For example, limited information about the assessment results can occur because the curriculum change is more recent and faculty are just beginning to examine their results.

In summary, when available, each example outlines the specific outcomes that faculty intend for students to achieve, the structure of the revised curriculum, and learning experiences and highlights of assessment results. These specific curriculum reforms represent changes that are designed to enhance students' communications (oral and written), problem-solving or critical thinking abilities and related dispositions, information competencies, or teamwork and collaboration.

The major curriculum reforms are drawn from undergraduate professional preparation programs in accounting, nursing, and education. Each area represents a different emphasis. Accounting is characterized as an enterprising field, nursing as a helping profession, and education as an informing profession (Stark, Lowther, and Hagerty, 1986). The challenges faced by the faculty teams profiled in this report are not unique to only these professional fields. The major curriculum changes highlighted in this chapter offer insightful lessons for faculty in many different disciplines, especially those who work with students in various professional fields.

Among the many external influences on curriculum development and reform are expectations that professional associations have established (such as the American Accounting Association) and explicit criteria promoted by professional accrediting associations (such as the American Assembly of

Collegiate Schools of Business). Although these external forces frequently shape curriculum innovations, they are not the sole reasons behind major changes in undergraduate education, and they do not necessarily generate faculty ownership of change. It is beyond the scope of this report to review in depth how external forces (such as accreditation) influence curriculum design. When faculty cite these external forces in their discussions of major changes in the curriculum, however, specific references are made to the appropriate influences.

Curriculum Reform in Accounting Programs

A recent national study of accounting education in undergraduate programs across the United States found that the majority of professional programs still have not addressed a number of major problems (Albrecht and Sack, 2000). The researchers found that the accounting curricula were too narrow and often outdated, and perceived to be driven by the interests of faculty and not by demands of the market. The majority of students were exposed to a rule-based model in which they were expected to memorize content to prepare for tests and the certifying public accountancy exam. Students were not prepared for the ambiguities that exist in businesses. In addition, they found that pedagogy typically focused on lectures that followed textbooks. These learning experiences did not help students to develop the ability to learn essential skills, nor did students have sufficient contact with businesses. Finally, the researchers reported that many accounting programs still focus "too much on content at the expense of skill development—skills students need to be successful professionals" (Albrecht and Sack, 2000, p. 45). Fewer than 25 percent of the department chairs who were surveyed indicated that they had totally revised their curriculum for accounting majors. These results echo similar findings from a comparative analysis of accounting education models that revealed changes over the past several decades have been minimal, with the majority of focus on entry-level knowledge needed for an accounting career (Needles and Powers, 1990).

Despite these results, some major reforms in accounting programs at selected colleges and universities are making a difference in student learning and development. Although changing the accounting curriculum may seem daunting to faculty, some groups of instructors have seriously undertaken major reforms in their programs with the intention of addressing the concerns outlined by numerous reports (for example, Albrecht and Sack, 2000; Big Eight Accounting Firms, 1989; Bedford, 1986). All reports stressed the importance of preparing accountants for their broadened functions, which include the identification and development of knowledge for a wide variety of decisions. In addition, there has been a uniform call for the need to emphasize communication, intellectual, and interpersonal skills. The Accounting Education Change Commission (AECC) and the Fund for the Improvement of Postsecondary Education (FIPSE) have often been key supporters of these curriculum innovations.

Some major reforms in accounting programs at selected colleges and universities are making a difference in student learning and development.

Because the following examples were often presented in the literature as in-depth case studies, each program and its changes are presented individually. Readers will then gain a stronger understanding of the context and the motivations for changing the curriculum and the reform process.

Project Discovery at the University of Illinois

The accounting faculty at the University of Illinois–Urbana-Champaign introduced comprehensive changes in both the content and form of the undergraduate accounting programs. Faculty were disappointed with their existing programs and believed that students did not possess the requisite skills of discovery—identifying problems, searching for information, and evaluating evidence. In today's dynamic environment, these types of skills are critical for successful professionals. The major goal of the revised curriculum was to change the instructional process from a focus mainly on content to "educating for expertise" by emphasizing the development of intellectual skills and attitudes (Stone and Shelley, 1997). The faculty wanted undergraduates to be provided with the necessary skills to develop their own expertise rather than solely creating accounting experts.

Professors and administrators reportedly "redesigned every undergraduate course by applying and adapting active learning and educating for expertise principles to accounting education" (Stone and Shelley, 1997, p. 38). The redesigned curriculum included an introductory sequence of accounting courses, five core courses organized around functional business concepts such as decision making and measurement, "an evolving set of courses designed to develop intellectual skills and professional attitudes," and elective courses that introduced undergraduates to important concepts in auditing, financial reporting, and taxation (Stone and Shelley, 1997, p. 38). Faculty added a skill component during the junior and senior years. Undergraduates were required to take a professional workshop for one credit hour over three semesters. These workshops specifically focused on developing communication skills, teamwork and leadership skills (including organization, negotiation, and conflict resolution), time management, stress management, interviewing, applied research skills (including reviews of databases and the Internet), and a focus on workplace issues (including discrimination, cultural diversity, and the global marketplace).

To facilitate this change, the accounting faculty hired a communications specialist as a lecturer and additional support staff (such as law students or English graduate students) to grade papers and work with Project Discovery (PD) students. The communications specialist was critical in helping faculty embed communication skills–related assignments into PD courses. Multiple-choice exams were replaced by written and oral communication assignments.

The accounting faculty did not immediately replace the entire curriculum at the beginning stages of their work. They implemented certain sections of each course on an experimental basis, giving students the opportunity to volunteer for these particular learning experiences. These experimental sections were then rigorously assessed to determine the impact of the curriculum changes compared with the more traditional course sections.

Faculty embedded specific approaches to learning across their accounting courses. First, they focused "on complex, ill-structured, ambiguous problems and cases similar to those found in the accounting practice" (Stone and Shelley, 1997, p. 38). Prior research indicated that undergraduates should be required to analyze contemporary issues in real-world settings that are representative of professional practice (Gardner and Motschenbacher, 1993). The goal was to provide students with simulated experiences that were sufficiently challenging and ambiguous enough that students would need to reflect fully on these key issues. Faculty also emphasized the development of intellectual skills and attitudes while deemphasizing the importance of memorizing facts, definitions, and vocabulary. Key intellectual skills included using knowledge to solve problems, differentiating and integrating alternative perspectives, identifying accounting-related information resources, structuring problem solutions, and building stronger communication skills.

Second, faculty decided to integrate active learning and team-oriented approaches across the redesigned accounting courses with the intention that students would develop stronger intellectual skills. Undergraduates were expected to identify and integrate diverse perspectives regarding ill-structured accounting problems and construct well-reasoned solutions. Students were also expected to work in teams and construct written as well as oral arguments. Faculty believed that learning would be more effective when students discovered knowledge by performing meaningful activities or projects.

Third, faculty deliberately structured repeated themes, materials, and cases that cut across accounting courses. Professors viewed repetition as a way to give undergraduates the opportunity to practice and refine their skills over time. Through these reinforcements, faculty hoped that student learning would be enhanced. Fourth, they created a social environment that they hoped would promote learning and innovation. Faculty encouraged students to become self-directed learners by fostering ongoing informal and formal interactions between practicing accounting professionals and undergraduate accounting majors. Finally, faculty changed their assessment strategies by evaluating student performance on ambiguous, complex cases and field projects rather than structured examinations and quizzes. They reviewed students' work and met to discern whether the learning activities provided insightful analyses and strongly reasoned decisions and conclusions rather than correct answers.

The accounting faculty consciously designed their courses to integrate more strongly and reinforce general education requirements. The faculty wanted students to develop stronger interpersonal and communication skills. Therefore, they embedded more team projects and written and oral reports.

Professors conducted multiple assessments that compared undergraduates in the traditional program with students in the Project Discovery curriculum. Through an analysis of syllabi and surveys of graduates, they found that faculty who taught PD courses made "greater use of expertise-building instructional processes such as field projects, case analysis, group work and presentations" (Stone and Shelley, 1997, p. 55). The traditional program made greater use of lectures and used examinations more heavily than the PD program. More than three-quarters of the PD graduates identified case analysis as the most frequently used instructional method, while four-fifths of traditional program graduates identified lectures by instructors as the dominant mode. PD students worked more frequently in groups and made more oral presentations than their counterparts. They found that PD students were better at identifying accounting information resources and ethical issues than were traditional program students. In addition, PD students demonstrated higher levels of cognitive complexity in analyzing issues in accounting. PD students also perceived that they had stronger communication and interpersonal skills than traditional program students. There were no significant differences in graduates' perceptions about the amount of work required in the PD program versus the traditional program.

Scores on CPA examinations revealed a few differences in students' performance. PD graduates achieved significantly higher auditing scores and showed evidence of stronger problem-structuring and writing skills as well as better attitudes than students in the traditional program. Faculty also discovered that PD students were in greater demand by recruiters for both internships and for permanent positions.

Integrating Liberal Learning Outcomes Across the Accounting Curriculum at King's College

The faculty at King's College believed that an undergraduate education should ideally help students to view learning as cumulative, transferable, and integrated. Therefore, faculty built on their general education program by explicitly embedding outcomes across their baccalaureate programs (Farmer, 1988). Undergraduates are expected to develop abilities in specific areas of liberal learning, including critical thinking, effective writing, effective oral communication, library and information literacy, computer literacy, and quantitative reasoning. Each group of faculty teaching specialized majors (including those in accounting) developed competency growth plans. These plans defined each transferable liberal learning skill in the context of the major or professional preparation program and then divided the skill into specific competencies. Undergraduates then ideally develop key skills in the general education core as well as their major courses. Each plan articulated an overarching definition of each skill, an indication of courses and assignments that were designed to help students master the particular skill, and specific criteria that faculty use to gauge the quality of students' work. These plans served as guides for both students and faculty, generating a greater understanding of how the curriculum was designed to foster the development of certain skills across learning experiences. These important skills were also reinforced in course syllabi and in instructions for assignments.

Faculty used primarily course-embedded assessments to determine whether students were reaching their goals. These assessments were intended to provide undergraduates with clearly defined expectations, personalized feedback on growth, and timely indications of areas needing attention (King's College, 1999). Professors created the sophomore-junior diagnostic project as a screening assessment to determine each student's ability in his or her major field of study regarding mastery of content and methods of the discipline. Faculty believed it also provided a meaningful assessment of the student's ability to apply the transferable liberal learning skills to a project in his or her major field of study (King's College, 1999).

The capstone feature of the curriculum was the senior integrated assessment. Faculty in each department designed an activity that asked students to demonstrate mastery of the subject matter and the methods of the major field as reflected in the departmental goals for liberal learning that were part of the competency growth plans. Students often made public presentations, exhibits, or lectures that other individuals and the public were invited to attend. All undergraduates completed this assessment, which served to demonstrate the students' readiness to function effectively and meet the expectations of employers and faculty members.

An example of the course-embedded assessment schedule is outlined in Table 1 for accounting majors at King's College. All the general education

TABLE 1
Schedule of Assessments for Majors in Accounting

General Education Outcomes	Freshman Year	Sophomore Year	Junior Year	Senior Year
Critical Thinking	CORE 100: Critical Thinking	ACCT 260: Intermediate Accounting I; ACCT 270: Intermediate Accounting II	ACCT 310: Advanced Accounting; ACCT 320: Cost Accounting	ACCT 410: Auditing
Effective Writing	CORE 110: Effective Writing	ACCT 270: Intermediate Accounting II	ACCT 310: Advanced Accounting	ACCT 420: Tax Accounting
Effective Oral Communication	CORE 115: Effective Oral Communication	ACCT 270: Intermediate Accounting II	ACCT 370: Accounting Information Systems	BUS 340: Business Law I; BUS 345: Business Law II
Library and Information Literacy	CORE 100: Critical Thinking; CORE 110: Effective Writing	ACCT 270: Intermediate Accounting II	ACCT 310: Advanced Accounting	ACCT 410: Auditing
Computer Competency	CORE 110: Effective Writing; BUS 121: Computer Applications in Business	ACCT 260: Intermediate Accounting I	ACCT 370: Accounting Information Systems	ACCT 420: Tax Accounting
Quantitative Reasoning	MATH 121: Calculus I	ACCT 270: Intermediate Accounting II	ACCT 320: Cost Accounting	ACCT 410: Auditing

SOURCE: King's College, Schedule of Assessments for Majors in Accounting. Reprinted with permission.

outcomes are linked with specific courses from the freshman year through the senior year. This plan includes assessments of certain skills in selected courses rather than an attempt to measure all skills in every course. In addition, this plan incorporates both general education courses and required learning experiences in the major in support of common outcomes. The accounting faculty also integrate the sophomore/junior diagnostic assessment in ACCT 270, Intermediate Accounting II, and ACCT 310, Advanced Accounting. The senior integrated assessment is embedded in ACCT 410, Auditing.

Across these course-embedded assessments, professors reported their results by describing the assessment activity, written criteria that were shared with students before the assessment, samples of students' work at three levels (superior, satisfactory, and less than satisfactory), proportions of undergraduates performing at each particular level, and how the assessment results were shared with other faculty. Through focus groups, students stated that they found course syllabi more detailed and directed toward learning; moreover, they liked knowing in advance the criteria that faculty would use to judge their performance (Farmer, 1999a). In addition, students believed that there were greater opportunities for them to have more meaningful interactions with faculty and that they were more aware of their sequential growth and development as learners (Farmer, 1999a). Students knew as freshmen that faculty in their major programs had clear expectations for them to transfer liberal learning skills to course work in their major discipline. Faculty reported that learning how to write criteria helped them to sharpen their own understanding as well as led to clearer objectives for student learning in the classroom.

Restructuring the Curriculum at Brigham Young University

The accounting program faculty at Brigham Young University (BYU) received a grant from the Accounting Education Change Commission to restructure the curriculum. They were concerned that students were too often required to memorize rules and procedures gained through lectures. "Concept applications were limited to textbook problems with only one right answer" (Albrecht and Associates, 1994, p. 402). Students did not get the opportunity to explore the relevance of accounting information to the real world, nor did they work in teams on projects. Although faculty asked students to write in a few accounting courses, the development of oral communications was reserved for graduate-level courses. Most of the curriculum consisted of separate functional courses; thus, faculty had little or no interaction with professors in different functional areas. They believed that the accounting curriculum had become fragmented and lacked continuity and integration.

BYU accounting faculty articulated three major goals for their curriculum reform efforts: identifying the competencies needed by professional accountants in the future; designing a curriculum to develop competencies in their undergraduates; and assessing whether students mastered these particular competencies.

Through a large field survey and a review of other competency studies, 27 important competencies were identified. About seven of these competencies were based on content and required students to acquire knowledge in accounting, auditing, taxes, and business. The majority of the other competencies were skill-based and had not been explicitly emphasized in the older accounting curriculum. These skills were clustered into five areas:

- *Written communication:* Ability to present views in writing;
- *Oral communication:* Ability to present views through oral communication and to listen effectively;
- *Group work and people skills:* Ability to understand group dynamics and work effectively with people, ability to resolve conflict, and ability to organize and delegate tasks;
- *Critical thinking:* Ability to solve diverse and unstructured problems; ability to read, critique, and judge the value of written work; and
- *Working under pressure:* Ability to deal effectively with imposed pressure and deadlines. [Albrecht and Associates, 1994, p. 408]

As the new curriculum was developed, each skill cluster became part of the focus of daily planning. The next two major steps the faculty focused on were changing the overall structure of the accounting program and reforming the curriculum and pedagogy during the junior year.

After serious deliberations, the accounting faculty decided to "fuse individual courses into an integrated, team-taught, 24 semester credit hour core" (Albrecht and Associates, 1994, p. 405). Teams of professors from systems, financial accounting, managerial accounting, tax and auditing, law, and international accounting planned, taught, and evaluated the core courses. This core integrated most of the traditional technical competencies and focused on nontechnical skills that were expanded on in the core. The accounting faculty also worked with a professor from the College of Education who helped instructors with identifying instructional weaknesses and in articulating an approach to reforming the curriculum.

In the foundation courses, undergraduates learned about key principles for different functional areas. They also were instructed about how to research issues and find solutions in the relevant literature. Once these courses were completed, the faculty team decided to use the business cycle approach to introduce students to various topics. The five major business cycles were sales/collection, acquisition/payment, payroll/performance evaluation, conversion/inventory, and financing (Albrecht and Associates, 1994). Faculty reported that all technical accounting concepts were integrated into the appropriate business cycle. Faculty believed that undergraduates understood how different events and problems required application of different functional areas and could more readily perceive the integrated connections among them. The business cycle helped undergraduates to examine all relevant aspects of a particular concept at the same time and encouraged a discussion of different perspectives on the same issue (Albrecht and Associates, 1994). The emphasis was on the role that accounting information had in management's decision processes.

All business students were required to complete a business writing course before enrolling in advanced accounting courses. The older accounting courses contained few writing assignments and examinations mainly comprised objective questions and short problems. Throughout the new core courses, accounting faculty integrated a series of short individual papers that they evaluated for content, grammar, and writing style. Undergraduates were expected to use writing to improve their learning experience by reflecting on a particular issue and then writing their responses often to case settings or business simulations.

In addition, students wrote three longer papers that consisted of research into a particular topic. Peers reviewed draft papers, and students had the opportunity to revise their papers before they turned in the final copy. Undergraduates also participated in groups where they were asked to divide writing responsibilities and to review each other's work before submitting a final draft. Writing skills were also emphasized on exams developed by faculty. They added essay questions and case study analyses to their evaluations of student learning.

Faculty required undergraduates to make formal presentations as well as informal communications such as discussions or debates. Students practiced their oral communication skills and listening through role playing and critiquing their own skills. All students also participated in an oral examination to assess their abilities to cope effectively with imposed pressures in an unstructured setting.

To enhance critical thinking skills, faculty designed unstructured problems that required students to integrate subject matter. Students critiqued and assessed numerous solutions for business problems. Examination questions were structured to ask students to explore problems through written analysis of very complex situations. Students also evaluated the work of their peers as individuals or in groups.

Group work was emphasized across the new junior core curriculum. Undergraduates met with business faculty for a day of instruction "about theory of group work, the principles of group dynamics, and the roles of various members of groups" (Albrecht and Associates, 1994, p. 410). Undergraduates participated in group assignments that were observed and critiqued by visiting professors.

Faculty believed that different instructional strategies were necessary because this new curriculum was based on an expanded set of expected skills. The courses were taught by professors in three-hour time blocks that helped faculty to include more group work in class as well as multiple opportunities for oral presentations and written work.

Senior administrators at BYU supported these major curricular reforms by providing release time and supplemental financial grants to participating professors who worked on this initiative. The BYU administration and faculty had typically stressed the importance of teaching by building a culture open to curriculum changes.

Preliminary assessment results revealed that students liked the new curriculum and believed that they were better prepared for their profession. Reactions of recruiters and senior administrators were positive and supportive. Most faculty viewed the curriculum in a positive light. However, some accounting faculty believed the future challenges include "a loss of autonomy and control, the lack of ownership of individual courses, the labor intensiveness of the program, a possible reduction in the amount of technical knowledge being learned by students, and the necessity of teaching in front of colleagues in a team-teaching environment" (Albrecht and Associates, 1994, p. 424).

Redesigning Intermediate Accounting Courses at the University of Virginia

The accounting faculty at the University of Virginia redesigned the curriculum in a manner similar to their BYU colleagues. Although their reforms were not as broad, they focused on a series of intermediate accounting courses. Accounting professors wanted to motivate students for their chosen profession, promote technical competencies, and develop an expanded set of skills, including the abilities to think critically, communicate, and conduct research (Catanach, Croll, and Grinaker, 2000). The faculty designed learning experiences that required undergraduates to be active participants in addressing unstructured real-world problems. Students researched these issues and developed "expert-like" thinking (Catanach, Croll, and Grinaker, 2000). The accounting faculty adopted a similar business-events systems approach as used by BYU to present undergraduates with accounting issues in a simulated business environment. Undergraduates were required to actively communicate in writing and orally the results of their work.

Student evaluations revealed that undergraduates found these redesigned courses to be demanding in terms of time and cognitive complexity (Catanach, Croll, and Grinaker, 2000). Students believed that there were strong features in the courses. They perceived that their learning increased, particularly in technical areas. They also valued the application of financial accounting to real-world scenarios. Students who graduated from this redesigned curriculum reported that they were well ahead of their peers in certain staff training courses. Accounting faculty who were teaching more advanced courses that rely on the experiences students gain in the intermediate courses reported that undergraduates were better prepared. The faculty reported that the emphasis on using accounting information for making business decisions had advanced student learning so that they can focus on more rigorous work in the upper-level courses. The faculty are planning a more comprehensive assessment of student learning that will include surveys and interviews with participants.

Reforming the Accounting Curriculum at Kansas State University

The accounting faculty at Kansas State University completed a comprehensive revision of the content and pedagogy in the curriculum. They followed nine major steps in their revisions:

- setting educational goals and objectives;
- developing an overarching framework based on the goals and objectives of the curriculum;
- identifying the accounting knowledge necessary for accounting professionals;
- establishing a set of criteria to determine the sequence of courses;
- creating a set of criteria for identifying the appropriate sequencing of content, skill development, and appropriate instructional strategies;
- designing course outlines that address the criteria and link with the framework;
- implementing new courses in the curriculum;
- evaluating the effectiveness of the new courses; and
- making necessary changes based on assessment results. [Ainsworth and Plumlee, 1993, p. 114]

The first overarching goal for the accounting faculty was to provide accounting students with sufficient technical and professional knowledge to form a basis for a successful career in accounting. They wanted undergraduates to understand, build on, and use their accounting knowledge. The second major goal was to provide accounting undergraduates with the skills necessary to use their knowledge in the business environment (Ainsworth and Plumlee, 1993). Faculty designed learning experiences expecting undergraduates to learn to cope with ambiguous circumstances and learn how to identify, evaluate, and select appropriate solutions to complex problems. Equally important was the ability to work effectively with others inside and outside the business environment. Finally, faculty wanted students to learn how to learn so that they could use information and new ideas throughout their professional careers (Ainsworth and Plumlee, 1993).

The accounting faculty used Bloom's taxonomy (1956) of cognitive objectives to formulate different levels of learning expectations for students. Lower-level accounting courses were designed to primarily address knowledge and comprehension with some focus on application (Ainsworth and Plumlee, 1993). The upper-level courses were created to address analysis, synthesis, and evaluation. Faculty also incorporated interpersonal skills across the upper-level accounting courses by requiring students to work in teams. They also built on their lifelong learning skills by working on professional research projects.

Accounting faculty used primarily the lecture method of teaching and objective testing in lower-level courses where the primary emphasis was on understanding knowledge. In the upper-level courses, professors used cases with oral and written assessments with an emphasis on enhancing students' problem-solving abilities. Formal assessments of student learning in the old curriculum compared with the new curriculum were in the beginning stages of development.

Changing the Curriculum at California State University–Chico
At California State University–Chico, the accounting faculty wanted to substantially revise introductory accounting courses in an effort to get more students to consider accounting as a potential major. A challenge in accounting education is that substantial attention is often given to using rules and procedures. As a result of this focus, some undergraduates lack the abilities to solve

unstructured problems and to make reasoned judgments and the interpersonal skills required to work effectively in teams.

With support from both AECC and FIPSE, the accounting faculty transformed the introductory courses into learning experiences that moved away from traditional coverage of topics to a structure centered on business decisions. Faculty designed their courses using the just-in-time decision case approach so that undergraduates would be exposed to accounting concepts as they would need them to address key business decisions or issues (Adams, Lea, and Harston, 1999). This approach was believed to help students gain a stronger understanding of important concepts by using practical applications. Groups of students were asked to analyze real-world cases using both quantitative and qualitative data. Each decision problem required students to learn new concepts in accounting, business, and organizations to solve the issue. The assignments required students to work in teams and moved the professor's role from a lecturer to a facilitator. As part of these learning experiences, students were also required to use word processing and spreadsheet software daily. The software was used to prepare accounting information for the purposes of decision making and was integrated into the introductory courses. These curriculum changes were designed to enhance students' abilities to make decisions in unstructured contexts when there was clearly no right answer.

Faculty implemented a set of formative assessment methods, including exit interviews, focus groups, and exit questionnaires to obtain detailed feedback from undergraduates enrolled in these new learning experiences. Undergraduates reported that collaborative learning activities and the active learning mode were working in terms of in-class group work and individual written reports. The faculty discovered that undergraduates were not clear about how their oral presentations would be evaluated and were distressed by the amount of group work outside class. Therefore, the faculty introduced explicit criteria by which students' oral presentations would be evaluated and significantly reduced the amount of group work required outside class. Results from attitude surveys given to students as pre- and postassessments revealed that undergraduates were increasingly positive about the effectiveness of their group work. They also reported they were increasingly proficient as writers and users of technology.

Summary of Reforms in Undergraduate Accounting Education

In accounting programs, it is evident that some groups of faculty have made considerable changes in an effort to improve student learning and preparation for their professional careers. All these examples demonstrate that accounting faculty have shifted their emphasis from teaching content only to a learning process that stresses important educational outcomes such as communication, interpersonal, and intellectual skills. As faculty revised their programs, they also reexamined their teaching and assessment practices. Professors tried new instructional strategies by deemphasizing the procedural complexities of accounting and stressing attention on substantive issues in the field. They used active learning approaches that encouraged students to work on problems under ambiguous circumstances, often in teams. They greatly expanded their use of case analyses, written assignments, class presentations, and small-group activities. Through these approaches, students had multiple opportunities to practice and build on important skills that encouraged them to be innovative and use creative approaches in addressing complex accounting problems or issues.

Curriculum Reform in Nursing Programs

Nurses in health care settings need to be effective critical thinkers as they strive to address multiple demands in changing environments. Rapid advances in science and technology, the expanding body of knowledge, and the dynamic health care delivery system require practitioners to think critically (Jacobs and Associates, 1997). A crucial criterion set forth by the National League for Nursing as one standard for measuring the quality of an educational program is the strength of its graduates' critical thinking skills (Poirrier, 1997).

In the past, nurses were often employed in hospital settings. More recently, however, "nurses have assumed such expanded roles as independent practitioners, managers in large health plans, and providers of alternative and complementary health care services" (Bellack and O'Neil, 2000, p. 15). These new roles impact the nursing curriculum and lead to calls for major reforms. Nursing practitioners often criticized those in nursing education for "distancing students from the real world of health care" (Cannon and Schell, 2001,

p. 167). The Pew Health Professions Commission issued its final report in 1998 and stressed that only through major transformations of professional education will health care professionals be ready to effectively assume their new roles. Knowledge and technical competencies continue to be important in preparing students for their work environments. However, "curricula must be redesigned to ensure that students have opportunities to acquire the broad general education competencies that will be demanded of them in practice. These include critical thinking and clinical judgement skills, effective organizational and teamwork skills, service orientation, cost awareness, accountability of clinical outcomes and quality of care, . . . and a commitment to continual learning and development" (Bellack and O'Neil, 2000, p. 16). For these skills to be strengthened, faculty should build innovations or major curriculum transformations that reorient "faculty, students, and the entire educational process to embracing the changing realities and demands of professional practice" (Bellack and O'Neil, 2000, p. 16). It is no longer sufficient to change the curriculum by randomly inserting new topics into a few courses or rearranging the sequence of courses. The survival of nursing programs is contingent on preparing students to practice effectively in today's challenging and dynamic health care environment (Cannon and Schell, 2001).

> **Undergraduates need multiple opportunities to achieve essential general education competencies that will be expected in the workplace.**

Nursing educators have often focused on the process of defining, implementing, and evaluating critical thinking skills in their programs as reported in the literature. A few examples are highlighted in this section that portray the key considerations and decisions that nursing faculty made as they reconsidered the purposes of their educational programs.

Defining Important Outcomes for Nursing Students
Some nursing faculty have focused on delineating outcomes and engaging their peers in formal discussions to identify the appropriate expectations for nursing students. However, these discussions may be representative of a small group of faculty. Videbeck (1997b) reported that in a sample of 55 nursing programs,

the majority of faculty provided mainly definitions of critical thinking that were global in scope, with only one program providing an operational definition of critical thinking.

A critical thinking model proposed by Videbeck (1997a) seeks to help faculty reconsider their educational goals. Key questions that should be answered as faculty deliberate about essential critical thinking skills for their students include:

- What does the program mean by critical thinking?
- How is critical thinking operationalized?
- What behaviors indicate use of critical thinking?
- What affective qualities should graduates possess? Can they be described in behavioral terms? Can they be measured?
- Can faculty agree on the operational definitions at least to the point that students get a clear and consistent message? [Videbeck, 1997a, p. 25]

Although it may be more time-consuming initially, nursing faculty as a group can answer these important questions and seek to reach a consensus about the most important critical thinking skills for their own graduates. Faculty have different assumptions about critical thinking that are revealed through open, ongoing dialogues about the essential dimensions.

The nursing faculty at a midwestern university undertook the challenge by defining essential critical thinking skills for undergraduates. Faculty reviewed the literature, held extensive discussions, and asked students to participate. Faculty considered several processes of critical thinking very important: "analysis: taking apart of information/data to find clues or patterns; evaluation: weighing the merit of data/information; decision-making: acting on the data/information or preparing for action; and synthesis: integrating information as a momentary end product or by product of the preceding cognitive activities" (Jacobs and Associates, 1997, p. 20). These activities culminated in a list of key indicators that represented important elements of critical thinking. Faculty will use these indicators in their future assessments of students' abilities.

Other nursing program faculty have developed in-depth competency statements that are intended to define the knowledge, skills, and abilities of nursing students. The Mississippi Council of Deans and Directors of Schools of Nursing developed a model that articulated its vision of nursing for students in the state (Eichelberger and Hewlett, 1999). A multilevel task force created a final document that was approved by the council. The document defined competencies for students based on three different nursing roles. The *provider* is a nurse who uses a systematic method, helps clients in meeting health care needs in a wide variety of settings, and coordinates the care of clients using a multidisciplinary approach (Eichelberger and Hewlett, 1999). The *member of a profession* is a nurse who is "accountable for ethical, legal, and professional dimensions of the practice of nursing" (p. 206). Finally, the *manager* is a nurse who uses resources to her or his fullest extent to achieve intended outcomes for the promotion of health in client populations. Each role has defined competencies that differ according to educational levels (whether students are completing their license, associate degree, baccalaureate degree, or master's degree). All nursing programs in the state have agreed to integrate information about the model into their curriculum. The intentions are that these competencies will be used in the development of new graduate and employee surveys that will assess competencies of new employees in the nursing workforce. Faculty may also use these competencies to guide curriculum design by planning learning experiences for the most appropriate level of nurse to deliver the most appropriate level of care (Eichelberger and Hewlett, 1999).

Transforming the Nursing Program to a Competency Model at the University of Memphis

The nursing faculty at the University of Memphis decided to move from a traditional program to a competency-based curriculum that required them to review all aspects of the major, including the beliefs, practices, and roles of faculty, administrators, and students (Luttrell and Associates, 1999). Faculty deliberately stated outcomes that were viewed as performance-based abilities necessary for contemporary practice in diverse settings and focused on essential professional responsibilities. They used these statements to guide their design of all learning experiences and as the basis for assessing student learning. Faculty revised each course to integrate outcomes, different learning strategies, and assessment. Four major questions guided this redesigned curriculum: "(1) What are the performance-based competency outcomes required for contemporary practice? (2) What are the measurable indicators of competence for each outcome? (3) What are the most effective learning strategies to achieve these outcomes? (4) What are the most effective methods to assess achievement of these competency outcomes?" (Luttrell and Associates, 1999, pp. 135–136).

Faculty intended to develop competencies that were realistic, practice based, and measurable. They viewed their work as a conceptual and operational redesign of the nursing program. They believed these competencies would ultimately serve as the framework for designing more meaningful interactive learning and enhanced performance assessment. The faculty adopted eight core competencies (including communication, critical thinking, and leadership) that were the basis for program and course outcomes across the curriculum. All nursing courses were designed to require increasing skill in all competencies as the content and clinical experiences became more advanced. Through this curriculum, students gained insights about the application of skills in clinical practice and increased both competence and confidence.

Faculty also created new learning strategies to enhance the achievement of each competency. They used more student-focused active strategies such as group exercises, projects, case studies, and simulations so that learning would be concentrated on competencies undergraduates would need to perform effectively in their actual work environments.

Faculty used competency and performance-based assessments for all courses and consistently evaluated outcomes as well as related skills across the curriculum. In particular, the nursing faculty used the competency performance (CP) assessment to gather evidence of student learning in the didactic, nonclinical courses required for nursing students. Examples of CP assessments included "writing . . . focused papers, nursing care plans, teaching plans, and a personal philosophy of nursing practice; critiquing research studies or articles on practice issues; making oral or poster presentations; conducting community health issues; and creating a budget" (Luttrell and Associates, 1999, p. 137). The CP examination was used to provide evidence of the clinical or client-related abilities most often assessed in laboratory and clinical courses. The assessment of these particular skills was based on specified critical elements that must be passed with total accuracy. Examples of CP examinations included "conducting a focused or comprehensive health assessment, implementing specific therapeutic interventions, monitoring or using technical equipment or procedures, teaching clients, and using leadership strategies in group situations" (p. 137). The CP examination was divided into two major components, a written assessment and a test of psychomotor skills. For the written component, nursing students had to assess a client's situation and make informed decisions about the appropriate care using a nursing care plan. Students viewed a short clinical videotaped vignette and then wrote the care plan to meet specific important elements related to diagnoses, including client-specific measurable outcomes for each diagnosis and appropriate nursing interventions to achieve client-related outcomes (Luttrell and Associates, 1999). Critical thinking was assessed further through the justification required for each nursing intervention. Students were confronted with clients who had pain or an infection or were immobilized.

To assess psychomotor skills, students were randomly assigned to perform a selected skill through a simulation with a client. Students learned about the types of patient problems and the range of skills that they should master during the examination. Students were tested on a random sample of these skills.

Faculty discovered that the competency approach to defining outcomes helped them to specify the essential knowledge and skills that are most important for their students. Instructors typically grapple with the underlying assumption that they must cover all the content. Through ongoing dialogue and collaboration, faculty reached a consensus about their most important expectations for student learning. Faculty believed that the teaching process and their class time were very focused and clearly related to nursing practice (Luttrell and Associates, 1999). Typically, faculty presented content in short segments followed by interactive application exercises. Professors believed this approach helped nursing students apply theory to practice in clinical settings.

Students reported that the new instructional strategies and classroom assessments help them to test their ideas and learn from peers. They expressed increased confidence in their knowledge and their ability to make decisions regarding patient issues (Luttrell and Associates, 1999).

Integrating Problem-Based Learning Across the Nursing Curriculum at the University of Delaware

For many years, problem-based learning (PBL) was implemented primarily in graduate-level programs, particularly medical education. However, it is a relatively new curriculum framework that is being adopted by faculty in selected undergraduate programs in the United States. At the University of Delaware, PBL was initially implemented across several undergraduate programs, including nursing. PBL has the potential to address several learning outcomes including the ability to "think critically and be able to analyze and solve complex, real-world problems; find, evaluate, and use appropriate learning resources; work cooperatively in teams and small groups; demonstrate versatile and effective communication skills, both verbal and written; and use content knowledge and intellectual skills acquired at the university to become continual learners" (Duch, Groh, and Allen, 2001, p. 6).

In addition to a focus on more advanced learning outcomes, PBL also requires the design of learning experiences in which students work in teams to solve complex real-world problems. Ideally, these learning experiences challenge students to find multiple resources that address dimensions of the problem and then evaluate the quality of the information as they review it. The outcomes associated with PBL are also linked with important information competencies. In the PBL environment, students initially need to determine the nature and extent of the information needed as they examine a particular problem or issue. Ideally, they also learn how to effectively and efficiently access information and how to critically evaluate it and its sources. These objectives reinforce important outcomes espoused by the Association of College and Research Libraries (2000).

PBL was originally considered by a small group of faculty who learned about its potential by participating in formal curriculum revisions of several courses connected with the Medical Scholars program, a collaborative initiative with Thomas Jefferson Medical College in Philadelphia. Eventually, this initial group of faculty grew and expanded curriculum reforms across selected undergraduate programs that were supported by senior administrators. This support included funds earmarked for PBL curriculum reform and an ongoing faculty development program including week-long events (Cavanaugh, 2001). Participating faculty and administrators believed they needed to transform undergraduate programs so that there would be an increasing emphasis on building strong inquiry-based learning experiences. It was expected that such learning experiences would help undergraduates reach more advanced outcomes.

At the University of Delaware, nursing students first gained experience with PBL in their required science courses. PBL was also integrated in both didactic and clinical nursing courses. The nursing content in each course "builds on knowledge, skills, and attitudes developed in the preceding courses, conducive to developing problems that are addressed over more than one course" (Cannon and Schell, 2001, p. 166). Because real-world problems were extended over several courses, faculty perceived that students learned and understood basic concepts that were then applied to the management of complex situations of increasing depth and breadth. Thus, the problems served as important bridges across courses, giving students the opportunity to also integrate knowledge from different fields and technical areas that relate to their major. Faculty intentionally planned learning experiences across their courses, hoping that students could develop knowledge and skills progressively. Professors built more advanced experiences across courses to reinforce learning. For example, in the learning labs that prepare students for clinical practice, undergraduates are often given complex scenarios that assess real-life situations that require the practice of psychomotor skills and communication skills needed before moving on to their clinical settings. The skills that nursing students master in the nursing labs are then applied to the practice setting. Clinical faculty and staff continue to promote stronger reasoning skills by asking students to "select the most pertinent data, identify and explain relationships among data, plan care, and evaluate appropriateness and effectiveness of care" (Cannon and Schell, 2001, p. 175). Students complete written assignments to demonstrate their understanding of data and relationships as well as how this information directs patient care.

In evaluating PBL experiences, undergraduates reported that the revised curriculum helped them "in reviewing for course and licensure exams, in learning focused history-taking and physical assessment, as well as for planning and implementing client and family education" (Cannon and Schell, 2001, p. 171). Nursing students believed they had a stronger confidence level and "competence in organizing new and managing complex information, preparation for more advanced conceptualization required for practice, and increased understanding, recall, and retention of content" (p. 171). Many students discussed their increased ability to systematically approach learning about health alterations (Cannon, 1998).

Weaving Information Literacy Across the Nursing Curriculum at San Francisco State University

Information literacy is an important skill for nursing students and directly links with their critical thinking abilities. For nurses to gain "the knowledge, skills, and attitudes necessary to value research-based practice and lifelong learning, schools of nursing must integrate information literacy into their curricula" (Verhey, 1999, p. 253). As clinical practice continues to become more complex, nurses will be confronted with increased information management challenges. Nurses will have to process and communicate more information than ever before, while the nature and types of information they handle will change (Travis and Brennan, 1998). A major challenge facing professors then is how to develop the abilities of nurses so that they can effectively use a wide range of information technologies and databases to make strongly reasoned judgments or decisions to address specific problems. The technical competencies for using computers are important; however, nurses need to learn how to critically appraise their information needs and then carefully critique various sources of information they gather to address patient care.

Breivik and Gee (1989, p. 24) define information literacy as "the ability to effectively access and evaluate information for a given need. It includes an integrated set of skills (research and evaluation) and knowledge of tools and resources." Information literacy is increasingly linked with critical thinking abilities. Students need to locate multiple sources of information that are relevant, accurate, and up to date as they strive to make informed decisions in ambiguous circumstances.

There may be some debate about the appropriate term, as some faculty may label similar sets of skills *information competencies*. One may argue that information literacy focuses on lower-level skills, but the discerning reader will note that the heart of this outcome (regardless of the specific label) rests with how each group of faculty defines it in their own setting. Breivik and Gee's definition (1989) clearly emphasizes the higher-order thinking abilities of evaluation and research. This is the definition that the nursing faculty at San Francisco State University (SFSU) adopted and adhered to as they changed their curriculum. Throughout this discussion, this outcome and the specific term are reported according to how the faculty of the curriculum reforms defined it for their own students.

A comprehensive needs assessment of both students and faculty was conducted at SFSU to identify their perceptions of "information literacy, to guide curriculum development, and to serve as baseline data for evaluating the information literacy strand" (Verhey, 1999, p. 253). Through this assessment, it was discovered that students believed they had weaknesses in their abilities to locate information and to evaluate it. They also reported a lack of knowledge, skills, and confidence in using computer databases, because they relied on textbooks as their main source of information. Faculty in their surveys confirmed these results and reported that students had difficulty critiquing and evaluating the information they did find.

San Francisco State University nursing faculty expected students to be able to demonstrate several skills: "individual knowledge, intellectual curiosity, and reasoning; a compassionate and empathic approach to people, with consideration of cultural backgrounds; a self-directed and creative approach to problems; knowledge and skills in nursing; and responsibility for high standards of nursing practice" (Verhey, 1999, p. 253).

Faculty conducted an extensive review and evaluation of the relevant literature in nursing and information literacy to establish a philosophical foundation for the key concepts and skills that would be incorporated in the nursing curriculum. Based on their evaluation, they decided to focus on two primary goals—the enhancement of critical thinking and learner empowerment. They then embedded specific information literacy objectives into nursing courses across the curriculum. Both theory courses and practicum learning experiences integrate information literacy concepts from the beginning of the major through the advanced required courses (see Table 2).

Faculty implemented a variety of new strategies into their nursing courses in an effort to develop stronger information literacy skills for their nursing students. "These strategies included specific instruction in the information explosion, the importance of lifelong learning in nursing, and the power of information and knowledge" (Verhey, 1999, p. 255). Beginning in the first course required for the major, faculty designed learning experiences that required students to use specific databases to electronically search for relevant information needed for specific assignments. In subsequent semesters, students were introduced to additional databases, and course assignments require students to use current literature related to nursing. Both individual assignments and group work required students to critique and evaluate the information they obtained.

The nursing faculty evaluated their curriculum reform efforts by surveying students and faculty before the literacy strand was implemented (referred to as *the 1992 sample*) and then after it was incorporated in their program in 1996. The students who participated in the new curriculum reported they used required textbooks significantly less often than the 1992 student sample (Verhey, 1999). In 1996, a statistically significant increase occurred in the use of a particular nursing database. This growth may have resulted because the nursing faculty increasingly emphasized this particular database to find information to support nursing theory and practice (Verhey, 1999). No significant change occurred in the two samples regarding their use of the SFSU library; however, the use of other libraries increased significantly for the 1996 sample of students, particularly the University of California at San Francisco. This large university research library supports schools of nursing and medicine as well as other related programs. A significant increase in its use may suggest that the new literacy strand is successful in encouraging students to use a variety of research-based information sources (Verhey, 1999). The 1996 sample reported a statistically significant increase in students' comfort level with using and evaluating information in academic journals and a decrease in accessing books. The faculty sur-

TABLE 2
Information Literacy Strand Outline

Theory Courses and Key Information Literacy Concepts	*Practicum Courses and Key Information Literacy Learning Experiences*
Semester I N111 Concepts of Professional Nursing N112 Healthy Aging and N114 Health Assessment • Importance of information literacy for lifelong learning in nursing; • Resources for nursing and health care information; • Relationship between clinical information and other resources.	*Semester I* N113 Practicum I—Geriatrics, Well Elderly • Use of more than one information resource in preparation of written assignments; • Use of current information in preparation of written assignments; • Use of information to support nursing assessments and interventions.
Semester II N222 Nursing of Adults N224 Technical Skills Laboratory N225 Pharmacology N333 Pathophysiology • Additional bibliographic databases; • Various literature search techniques; • Beginning evaluation of information.	*Semester II* N223 Practicum II—Adults • Evaluation and use of multiple information sources in written assignments; • Integration of patient information and information from nursing and health care resources.
Semester III N334 Family Assessment and Maternity Nursing N336 Nursing Care of Ill Children • Evaluation of information • Using literature in clinical practice.	*Semester III* N335 Practicum III—Maternity N337 Practicum IV—Pediatrics • Use of computerized nursing network via computer in multimedia lab; • Incorporation of filtered literature in written assignments; • Application of nonresearch literature findings in clinical practice.

TABLE 2
(Continued)

Theory Courses and Key Information Literacy Concepts	Practicum Courses and Key Information Literacy Learning Experiences
Semester IV	*Semester IV*
N444 Psychiatric Mental Health Nursing	N445 Practicum V—Psychiatric Mental Health
N446 Community Health Nursing	N447 Practicum VI—Community Health
• Application of nursing and health care research to complex clinical problems;	• Use of research literature in preparation of written assignments;
• Advanced information-seeking and evaluation techniques.	• Use of research findings in actual clinical practice.
Semester V	*Semester V*
N555 Nursing Research	N557 Practicum VII—(Senior Clinical of Choice)
N556 Nursing Leadership	
• Critical synthesis of research literature;	• Minireview of literature on topic related to clinical specialty;
• Information networks for nursing research applications;	• Analysis of computer applications in clinical and management practice.
• Health care management information systems;	
• Database management systems for "bedside" clinical practice.	

SOURCE: Verhey, M. P. "Information Literacy in an Undergraduate Nursing Curriculum: Development, Implementation, and Evaluation." *Journal of Nursing Education*, 1999, *38*(6), p. 254. Reprinted with permission.

vey results tended to support and expand on these findings. Professors believed that the 1996 sample showed improvements in using outside readings to support assigned projects. In 1992, more than two-thirds of the faculty believed that students were missing specific information literacy skills, while in 1996, only about one-third of the faculty indicated undergraduates were lacking specific information skills (Verhey, 1999). The faculty believed that nursing students in 1996 demonstrated improvement in using current information in course assignments, but they believed that some students still had difficulties in evaluating the quality of the information that was located. This finding suggested to the faculty that although some improvements were being made, there is an area of critical thinking that is important to focus on in the future—how to evaluate multiple sources of information.

Integrating Informatics into the Nursing Curriculum at Case Western Reserve University

The nursing faculty at Case Western Reserve University designed, implemented, and evaluated *nursing informatics* across four required nursing courses. The concept is very similar to information literacy, except that an interdisciplinary approach is used to address the topic. Nursing informatics is a "combination of computer science, information science, and nursing science designed to assist in the management and processing of nursing data, information, and knowledge to support the practice of nursing and the delivery of nursing care" (Graves and Corcoran, 1989, p. 228). The four-course sequence addresses both conceptual and technical skills.

Because a limited number of faculty were familiar with this concept, special strategies such as peer coaching and role modeling were used to help instructors gain knowledge and expertise regarding nursing informatics. In addition, external consultants who were experts on the topic delivered one- to two-day conferences for participating faculty. Instructors received support to attend conferences. As this curriculum reform was implemented, student mentors and clinical teaching associates also attended conferences to help them better understand the new ideas.

The three major components of the curriculum framework used by the nursing faculty focused on information, technology, and clinical care across the four courses. The primary objective in the initial NURS 120 (Nursing Informatics I, Introduction) course is to provide students with "a basic understanding of the flow of information through the health care environment and the ways in which information technology can facilitate collecting, processing, and communicating this information" (Travis and Brennan, 1998, p. 164). In the second course, NURS 222 (Nursing Informatics II), students learn how to access, document, and critically analyze computerized patient care records. Students work on a computerized hospital simulation program, which gives them the opportunity to apply classroom concepts to technology. In the third course, NURS 345 (Nursing Informatics III), students "use information technologies to support nursing management in clinical applications" (Travis and Brennan, 1998, p. 165). The expectation is that students will gain a stronger understanding of the relationships between nursing applications and computer applications used across a hospital, and the impact of nursing interventions on other information-processing systems with different departments. Students also "examine the process of planning, designing, developing, implementing, and evaluating nursing information systems in a clinical environment" (Travis and Brennan, 1998, p. 165). The final course, NURS 346 (Nursing Informatics IV), builds on the knowledge gained in previous courses to create a perspective on the adoption and use of nursing information systems to help nurses make decisions. Students work in teams of five to seven members to address a real-world issue or problem with a specific agency. Therefore, these projects stem from real needs in an actual hospital environment. All the projects challenge students to collaborate with an agency staff member to define outcomes and project products, interact with peers in a very focused manner, and apply prior nursing informatics knowledge to solve real-world problems.

The nursing faculty evaluated this new curriculum by assessing student performance, getting feedback from employers, and using course evaluations. Student evaluations of these new courses ranged from enthusiastic to discouraging. Some students questioned these courses despite students' beliefs that course objectives were attained. They wanted a strong textbook to use rather than a compilation of articles. When the nursing faculty implemented this curriculum, however, most textbooks focused on computer applications rather than a more comprehensive approach. In surveys, students reported that they became more realistic than idealistic in their evaluations of information technology in nursing. Employers' reactions were positive; they indicated a decrease in the amount of time needed to orient new employees. In most cases, new graduates were able to effectively use the information resources available to them.

Summary of Reforms in Nursing Education

The nursing curriculum reforms clearly demonstrate the major changes that faculty made to create a learner-centered curriculum. Professors wanted students to become stronger critical thinkers and make informed decisions that are relevant to real-world problems. The nursing programs discussed here emphasize critical thinking and problem solving, which are sometimes linked with information literacy. Professors carefully articulated higher expectations for student learning and then designed learning experiences that directly addressed these outcomes. They also experimented with new instructional approaches that often emphasized active learning and teamwork. In addition, undergraduates frequently worked on complex, open-ended real-world problems. Instructors tried new assessment approaches that moved professors away from relying only on multiple-choice tests to demonstrations of student performance and abilities through cases, simulations, written assignments, and oral presentations. Students often reported greater confidence in their own abilities as well as stronger preparation for their new positions in the workplace.

Curriculum Reform in Teacher Education Programs

For many years, teaching in elementary and secondary schools was treated as a form of semiskilled labor requiring mainly the ability to get through the book with the aid of a few routine procedures (Darling-Hammond, 1999). A common criticism of teacher education programs is that they lack rigorous course work and intellectual challenge (Romanowski and Oldenski, 1998). Certain recurring issues are associated with relevance of course work and its redundancy, the lack of critical thinking abilities, and weak role models in both college faculty and classroom teachers (Applegate and Shaklee, 1992). Some employers believe new graduates who enter the teaching profession are not prepared with the practical knowledge and skills they need to perform effectively in their new roles. Critics believe that theory is separated from practice and that deep learning about complex issues or problems in the real world is thus neglected. Courses in teacher education programs have become fragmented and often have very little relationship with one another (Tom, 1997). This fragmentation continues as a result of increasing specialized knowledge and individual departments that have control over distinct courses. "Courses on subject-matter topics have become disconnected from courses on teaching methods, which have become disconnected from courses on learning and development" (Darling-Hammond, 1999, p. 31). Many learning experiences in teacher education are not grounded in a common set of educational purposes, themes, or assumptions (Tom, 1997), leading some critics to believe that teacher education programs have no direction or too many directions, with individual students charting their own path. These issues are very similar to those espoused in undergraduate accounting and nursing programs.

Promising New Programs in Teacher Education: Results from Evaluation Studies

Increasingly, more attention and importance are placed on the expertise of the nation's teachers. Promising new programs have undergone major reforms in an effort to change the conditions existing in teacher education programs. Faculty in some schools of education are creating programs that extend beyond the traditional four-year degree program and include strong relationships with local schools (Darling-Hammond, 1999). These revised programs require students to receive a strong disciplinary background and extensive study of teaching and learning that is integrated with intensive clinical training in schools. Some colleges offer one- or two-year graduate programs, others a five-year model that allows for an extended preparation program for prospective students who are undergraduates pursuing a major in teacher education. The fifth year of these teacher education programs helps undergraduates to focus their last year solely on preparing to teach and gaining experience in school-based internships connected to course work on teaching and learning (Darling-Hammond, 1999). Many of these programs are collaborating with local school districts to create professional development schools that plan students' clinical preparation. Similar to teaching hospitals in medicine, these schools provide sites for "state-of-the-art practice that also train new professionals, extend the professional development of veteran teachers, and sponsor collaborative research and inquiry" (Darling-Hammond, 1999, p. 31).

The National Commission on Teaching and America's Future assessed several innovative teacher education programs and found that they have several distinct features in common (Darling-Hammond, 1999 and 1997). First, a clear vision of good teaching was apparent in all course work and clinical experiences. Program faculty had reached agreements about what good teaching was and built a series of courses and experiences that ensured that building blocks for teaching were present and reinforced (Darling-Hammond, 1999). The faculty demonstrated an ethical commitment to the education of all students along with the development and application of teaching strategies that address the needs of a wide range of students (Darling-Hammond, 1999). Second, faculty articulated explicit and specific standards constituting what teachers should know and be able to do to teach their subject matter to diverse groups of students. They used these standards to guide and evaluate course work and clinical experiences.

"Teachers-in-training experience many examples of the kind of practice they are trying to develop as well as many opportunities to get feedback about their progress" (Darling-Hammond, 1999, p. 32). Third, faculty developed a rigorous core curriculum that consisted of a systematic program of study grounded in the substantive knowledge of the content that a teacher needs to know and teach in the context of practice (Darling-Hammond, 1999). In addition, faculty extensively used problem-based learning methods, including case studies, research on teaching issues, performance assessments, and portfolio evaluation (Darling-Hammond, 1999). These particular methods were found to help students apply principles and theories to real-world problems as they learned to think about how to address key issues. Fourth, faculty developed intensively supervised, extended clinical experiences (typically at least 30 weeks) that were designed to support what students learned in their courses. Undergraduates worked closely with master teachers in school settings that helped build strong bridges between theory and practice. Students gained opportunities to apply their classroom learning to these real-world settings. Finally, strong relationships and partnerships were formed with local schools that were open to major reforms or had already implemented dramatic changes. These partnerships supported "the development of common knowledge and shared beliefs among school- and university-based faculty"

(Darling-Hammond, 1999, p. 32). Ultimately, these schools became sites for "state-of-the-art practice, training, and research" (p. 32).

Trinity University is a liberal arts college that illustrates some of these major curriculum reforms. The school replaced a traditional four-year education major with a five-year program that combines a bachelor's degree in an academic discipline with a master of arts in teaching (Darling-Hammond, 1999). Professors in liberal arts and teacher education work together on courses that integrate intensive study in the discipline and the study of pedagogy for teaching key concepts with modes of inquiry in the field. For example, potential elementary school teachers can take their bachelor's degree in humanities, a field designed specifically for the master's in teaching program. Students work on completing integrated, carefully planned education courses, including 135 hours of clinical experiences in the university's partner schools. These courses are designed "to help students understand children and their development, schooling and its purposes, learning and cognition, the influences of culture and context, and effective teaching strategies for all children, including those with disabilities" (Darling-Hammond, 1999, p. 31). In the fifth year, students complete a one-year internship in a professional development school collaborating with expert teachers and professors at Trinity. Through their course work, students apply their academic knowledge to real problems by working with their teachers to reform the instruction at their schools. For example, one of the professional development schools had experienced high student mobility and low achievement. To address this problem, an education team from Trinity created a program "in which students progress through the grades as a single group while teachers use common methods derived from their analyses of educational research. Within a few years, test scores among students in the program had climbed, while the student mobility rate, which was 59 percent elsewhere in the school, declined to 2 percent" (Darling-Hammond, 1999, p. 32). Local school administrators perceive that graduates from Trinity's new five-year program are well prepared for their new professional roles. The University of Cincinnati, the University of Connecticut, Michigan State University, and the University of Virginia are some of the major universities that are following Trinity's example.

Researchers have found that graduates of these extended programs are more satisfied with their preparation and are also perceived by their colleagues, principals, and cooperating teachers as better prepared (Darling-Hammond, 1999). They are more likely to enter and remain in teaching than their peers who attended a traditional four-year program. They are also as effective with students as more experienced teachers.

Defining Important Competencies and Using Exhibitions of Performance in Teacher Education at Alverno College

Alverno College faculty have followed an ability-based undergraduate curriculum since the early 1970s that includes the professions (such as business and nursing). The key outcomes that faculty expect undergraduates to develop through their learning experiences include communications, analysis, problem solving, valuing in decision making (the ability to understand the moral dimensions of decisions and to accept responsibility for the consequences of actions taken), social interaction (the ability to get things done in groups), global perspectives (the ability to articulate interconnections between and among diverse opinions, ideas, and beliefs about global issues), effective citizenship, and aesthetic responsiveness. Each outcome provides a framework or a curriculum plan for students to work effectively with the subject matter of their courses (Mentkowski and Associates, 2000). As students gain experience and become more sophisticated, they draw on various abilities that they have developed and combine them in more advanced ways (Mentkowski and Associates, 2000).

The faculty at Alverno College created a series of developmental levels that correspond to a student's progression across the entire curriculum. For each level of ability, they developed specific criteria that characterize mastery. For example, students were expected to develop facility in problem solving by demonstrating certain levels of performance. At each level, using any or all parts of a problem-solving process meant that undergraduates defined the problem, analyzed information, selected and implemented a strategy, and evaluated their solutions. The six levels of performance included:

- *Level 1:* Articulation of one's own problem-solving process, making explicit the steps taken to approach the problem(s);

- *Level 2:* Analysis of the structure of discipline- or profession-based problem-solving frameworks;
- *Level 3:* Use of discipline- or profession-based problem-solving frameworks and strategies;
- *Level 4:* Independent examination, selection, use, and evaluation of various approaches to develop solutions.

Two other levels applied to majors and areas of specialization:

- *Level 5:* Collaboration in designing and implementing a problem-solving process;
- *Level 6:* Solving problems in a variety of professional settings and advanced disciplinary applications (Mentkowsi and Associates, 2000, pp. 420–421).

In addition to these general education abilities, undergraduates pursuing the teacher education program are expected to develop five additional professional education abilities:

- *Conceptualization:* The ability to integrate content knowledge with educational frameworks and a broadly based understanding of the liberal arts to plan and implement instructions;
- *Diagnosis:* The ability to relate observed behavior to relevant frameworks to determine and implement learning strategies;
- *Coordination:* The ability to manage resources effectively to support learning goals;
- *Communication:* The ability to use verbal, nonverbal, and media communication to establish the environment of the classroom and to structure and reinforce learning; and
- *Integrative interaction:* The ability to act with professional values as a situational decision maker to develop students as learners. [Alverno College, 1996, p. 2]

Faculty integrate the development of these abilities across the teacher education curriculum and embed them in "the contexts of learners' developmental needs, an appreciation for diversity, a view of professionalism that includes ongoing inquiry to inform teaching, a concern for democratic education, and a commitment to the use of media and technology" (Darling-Hammond and Snyder, 1998, p. 271). Furthermore, they articulate these expectations for the beginning teacher, for the developing teacher with classroom experience, and for the experienced professional teacher. Faculty use these expectations in the assessment of students' abilities.

The faculty redesigned all course work, field experiences, and assessments to emphasize the development of the key knowledge, skills, dispositions, and attitudes associated with their expectations. All the course syllabi at Alverno articulate the specific developmental levels of specific abilities they address. Faculty outline learning activities and assessments in their syllabi.

Program faculty assess their outcomes by students' performance on multiple measures, including essays, letters, position papers, case study analyses, observation of events, talks to simulated audiences, productions of videos and curriculum materials, and simulated events such as parent-teacher conferences (Darling-Hammond and Snyder, 1998). The judgments of cooperating teachers, college supervisors, employers, and undergraduates themselves indicate that graduates are very self-reflective and strongly prepared for their professional positions.

Merging Content and Pedagogy Across the Teacher Education Program at Missouri Western State College

The education faculty at Missouri Western State College restructured the teacher education program to emphasize the integration of content and pedagogy. Specifically, they sought to create higher-quality learning experiences for their undergraduates by getting students to engage in ongoing reflections about their work. Faculty also wanted to achieve a more balanced perspective between pedagogy and content within and across all the teacher education courses. In mathematics, the faculty changed the curriculum by shifting the focus from only doing problems to promoting thinking about mathematical concepts by having students write their own explanations of how they solved problems. Students learned tasks by watching their peers rather than instructors modeling them. The faculty also integrated similar processes in their language arts courses. Students are required to complete writing activities that "critically examine the assumptions and beliefs of pre-service candidates and explore new perspectives on what it means to be a teacher" (Edwards, 1997, p. 48). The language arts instructors collaborate with colleagues in liberal arts and sciences, including the director of Writing Across the Curriculum, who is also an English professor. A four-part project requires students to study critical issues through the publication of case studies; students produce an investigative report on a research question that arises from the questions raised during the case studies.

Assessment results indicate that undergraduates who participated in the new curriculum performed in the upper ranges of the National Teachers Exam (Edwards, 1997). Evaluations of teachers by principals indicate that students in the new curriculum were ranked as the best when compared with other novice teachers. The faculty plan to conduct additional analyses.

Developing Professional Teachers at the University of Florida

A variety of external factors calling for major change created an environment in the University of Florida's teacher education program in which curriculum reform became essential. Faculty were troubled by the increasing national and state perception that "quality of teaching and particularly of teacher education was low" (Ross and Bondy, 1996, p. 68). The expanded knowledge base for teacher education was not integrated into teacher education programs. As enrollments declined in the College of Education, state legislators questioned the need for colleges of education in Florida's state universities and considered abolishing them. All these factors stimulated a strong need for major reform.

The development of a new five-year teacher education curriculum was guided by the college dean and supported by the vice president for academic affairs. The faculty created a steering committee that was responsible for developing the plan for change and its major tasks. Major structural changes included "[1] provision of a five-year program leading to a master's degree and/or teacher certification, [2] an increase in the length and quality of liberal arts and science content, [3] expansion of foundational and clinical studies, [4] an emphasis on research-based knowledge about teaching and learning,

[5] development of professional expertise in elementary education and a second professional area, and [6] an increase in admission and retention requirements" (Ross and Bondy, 1996, p. 64). The development of teachers' reflective judgment became the central goal that cut across the curriculum. Faculty reached an agreement about the key criteria used to evaluate reflective judgment that was shared with students in their handbook:

- Ability to recognize educational dilemmas;
- Willingness to assume responsibility for educational decisions;
- Ability to view situations from multiple perspectives;
- Ability to evaluate real or potential consequences of a decision;
- Ability to search for alternative explanations for events occurring in the classroom;
- Use of adequate evidence to support a position or decision;
- Willingness to consider new evidence; and
- Ability to judge the adequacy of a decision or position based on the context of application. [Ross, Johnson, and Smith, 1992, p. 27]

Faculty viewed reflection as an integrated construct and assessed both the content and process of reflection in their research. They introduced undergraduates to reflective teaching in their first semester. Then across the curriculum, professors used a variety of activities, including reflective writing, curriculum development and analysis, action research projects, and faculty modeling (Ross and Bondy, 1996). To maintain a focus on reflective teaching, faculty developed core courses to increase programmatic coherence, trained supervisors of field experience, and helped graduates establish a network to support each other.

Formal research studies designed to evaluate the impact of this new program have found that "some students and graduates are moderately or highly reflective and at least some maintain their reflective abilities during the first year of teaching" (Ross, Johnson, and Smith, 1992, p. 36). Students reported the program was a positive influence on the development of their perspectives and abilities as teachers, while principals viewed the program's graduates as competent.

The Academically Talented Teacher Education Program at Kent State University

Kent State University faculty designed the Academically Talented Teacher Education Program (ATTEP) to address the need for stronger preparation of teachers and to retain high-quality professionals who would remain working in schools for longer periods of time. This alternative program sought to recruit and retain academically talented students who demonstrated superior performance over their peers. Students were identified by grade point average, standardized test results, evidence of critical thinking, and complexity in oral and written expression (Applegate and Shaklee, 1992). In addition, "the ability to plan and do independent work; ability to understand, analyze, and synthesize key concepts; interpersonal communication skills; leadership potential; commitment to teaching; and breadth of life experiences" were considered (Applegate and Shaklee, 1992, p. 69).

This alternative program developed several features:

- Emphasis on inquiry across courses;
- Identification of a cohort group;
- Identification of mentor teachers to work with undergraduates for an extended period of time;
- Incorporation of action research in the culminating internship as a strategy for verifying acquisition of an inquiry approach to teaching;
- Faculty teams used to teach courses and share perceptions; and
- Analysis and evaluation of data about participating students and the entire program.

Faculty believed that teachers' work is often ambiguous and uncertain (Applegate and Shaklee, 1992). Therefore, the development of reflective inquiry abilities for participating students was defined as encouraging students to ask questions about their own practices, those of the faculty members, and those of their mentors. It also included helping students learn how to make reasoned choices and to develop a reflective style that was conceptually flexible. The primary challenge in this program was "to bring together [a] desire to stimulate reflection in teacher candidates by stimulating conceptual development through providing different kinds of information about teaching, learning, and schooling with complex problem-solving tasks derived from conceptually different views of knowledge" (Applegate and Shaklee, 1992, p. 69).

Each new cohort of undergraduates began in the fall semester by enrolling in a seminar entitled Inquiry into Teaching. Each student worked with a mentor and gained real-world experience working with this teacher over three semesters. Additional inquiry-based seminars included Inquiry into Learning, Inquiry into Schooling, and Research into Teaching. Across the education courses, students were encouraged to regularly measure, evaluate, and sort information and knowledge in relation to their own values, ideas, and conceptions of teaching (Applegate and Shaklee, 1992). Faculty modeled the inquiry strategies so students learned how to challenge the professor and others to be clear about the beliefs that influence their practice. Students wrote in reflective journals and analyzed their own learning process. They also actively engaged in the classroom as faculty created activities that required them to try new and innovative strategies for addressing classroom problems. During their final semester, students created and implemented their own action research project and identified a problem to study.

Faculty designed a comprehensive program evaluation by using multiple methods. ATTEP students were given the Measure of Epistemological Reflection instrument before entering the program and again as they completed it. This measure, the only standardized instrument used, assesses the development of cognitive complexity. Results indicated a continual development of cognitive complexity for ATTEP students. Videotaped class sessions were analyzed by faculty. They found that "students actively participated in structuring sessions, provided experiential examples to extend discussions, asked substantive questions of each other and professors, and evaluated their peers and professors' statements" (Applegate and Shaklee, 1992, p. 74).

The capstone learning experience for all interns at the end of their program is the Learning to Teach Autobiography. Students complete a series of questionnaires and include their journals. They also write their responses to twelve open-ended questions about "past, present, and future career experiences, including commitment to teaching; changes to self, knowledge, and learning; problems and conflicts encountered in all aspects of the learning to teach process; specific examples of indirect and direct learning, and future directions" (Applegate and Shaklee, 1992, p. 75). An analysis of the information and data gleaned from this capstone experience showed that students achieved the abilities to self-reflect, reflect on the practice of teaching, including making connections between theory and practice, and analyze critical issues affecting the profession.

Summary of Reforms in Teacher Education

The examples of major curriculum reforms in professional education discussed in this section clearly reveal that many of these groups of faculty adhered to certain good practices as they changed learning experiences for students. These good practices are consistent with the major calls for reform in undergraduate education suggested by the Education Commission of the States (1995, 1996). Faculty members spent considerable time and effort reconceptualizing their expectations for student learning. They worked in teams as they made important decisions. Professors shifted their emphasis from a focus solely on delivering content to using content to help students develop stronger reasoning, communication, and problem-solving skills. They developed higher expectations that were attainable. Typically, professors articulated their learning outcomes before they taught students. Faculty members created clear learning outcomes for the entire program and then linked these outcomes to individual courses that were designed to achieve their expectations.

Some faculty realized that they were not experts in designing new learning experiences for students that focused on the development of certain outcomes. Therefore, they formed crucial partnerships with colleagues on campus who possessed expertise in these areas. For example, they formally worked with the English faculty, speech communication faculty, librarians, and advanced graduate students. These collaborations crossed disciplinary boundaries and helped faculty in the professions to build stronger learning experiences by emphasizing the most critical dimensions of student learning and then reinforcing these outcomes across numerous courses.

Faculty often created strong curriculum models that tightly linked general education outcomes with course work in the major. At some colleges, all general education or liberal learning outcomes were stressed across the entire curriculum, from the freshman through the senior year. Faculty consciously planned the entire curriculum to promote these outcomes over time. They gave students multiple opportunities to practice and refine their skills in different contexts. For example, although critical thinking was often a required course for general education, faculty teaching specialized major courses typically required students to demonstrate advanced critical thinking skills in numerous upper-division courses. Undergraduates then had the opportunity to use their knowledge to address key issues or problems that were important in their chosen professional preparation program.

Professors also identified important cycles of decision making and implemented projects or cases that cut across several courses in the major. In this way, students had the opportunity to examine complex problems through multiple perspectives. Such initiatives encouraged faculty to work in teams to create more purposeful and integrated learning experiences.

Because faculty consciously planned their curriculum by articulating student outcomes and assessing their expectations, a more coherent curriculum was delivered. Students knew early what was expected in terms of their performance, and they were given criteria regarding expectations for various assessments. Often multiple assessments required students to draw on their knowledge and apply it to a real-world problem or issue. Faculty often gave students the freedom to design their own projects linked to their interests and the goals of their education programs. Faculty members found these assessments often provided meaningful data to guide future curriculum development and reform. Although many assessments were of courses, others evaluated the program that led to suggestions for improvements.

Students were challenged to advance multiple skills in communications, problem solving, and critical thinking. Although it was still important for students to gain new knowledge and understand it, undergraduates needed to apply or use that knowledge in the reformed curriculum to solve complex problems or issues that were often relevant for their particular profession.

Undergraduates were actively engaged in their learning, often completing assignments such as projects, papers, or exhibitions that helped them to synthesize the knowledge, abilities, and skills they learned from the freshman year through their senior year. Undergraduates frequently were required to work together in teams to solve real-world issues or problems. As students explained their learning to their peers, they often found that they better understood the material and were exposed to new ideas that they had not considered before their teamwork.

Faculty tended to provide students with frequent feedback about their performance. Traditionally, professors assigned grades for student work. Faculty members in the reformed curriculum, however, used authentic assessments to determine the quality of a student's performance and work. Overall, faculty implemented multiple assessments that provided useful information on which to make decisions about targeted changes to enhance student learning.

Implementing and
Assessing Internships

A CHALLENGE FOR HIGHER EDUCATION, particularly faculty responsible for professional preparation programs, is to prepare new graduates to more effectively make the transition from college to their new full-time professional positions. Even students who hold jobs throughout their enrollment in college find the shift to the workplace upon graduation to be a significant transition as a result of new roles and expectations (Holton, 1998).

Major differences exist between the cultures of college and work (Holton, 1998). Typically, college students get regular feedback about their performance through grades and comments from faculty and peers. They usually participate in highly structured professional preparation programs that provide a great deal of direction. They have flexible schedules with few major changes. College students get frequent breaks and time off and more control over their time and the interests they pursue. They focus on their own development and growth, with opportunities to create and explore knowledge often through individual efforts.

Feedback in the workplace is infrequent and less precise (Holton, 1998). Employees usually work in highly unstructured environments and engage in tasks that have few directions. They experience less personal support than in college and also encounter frequent and unexpected changes. Employees have limited time off and work with structured schedules. They work under supervision and respond to delegated responsibilities. They are expected to demonstrate results with their knowledge by applying it to complex problems or issues that often have very few right answers. They work in teams to get results for the organization that require a great deal of initiative. Despite the major differences between college and work environments, there are ways that undergraduates can engage in learning experiences to more effectively prepare them for the transition to the workplace.

Learning from experience provides students with opportunities to analyze their own work as learners in a variety of formal and informal contexts. Internships are one form of experiential learning that has the potential to enhance undergraduates' intellectual, personal, and ethical growth (Smith, 1998). In a national study, college internship coordinators identified the types of skills that interns develop through their on-site learning experiences (Page, Geck, and Wiseman, 1999). The skills most frequently developed include thinking critically, dealing with the pressures of professional work, applying their classroom learning, working on challenging duties and assignments, gaining a perceived edge in the job market, learning about real-world politics in the workplace, enhancing their communication skills, clarifying their career direction, and learning to work in teams. These results reinforce another study in which students reported that internships enhanced their communication and interpersonal skills needed for negotiating, working with others, and working in teams (Raymond and McNabb, 1993).

Through internships, students also learn to reflect on their own experiences as valid data for understanding their actions, provided they receive guidance (Cromwell, 1993; Grantz and Thanos, 1996; Hutchings and Wutzdorff, 1988). Internships can provide students with meaningful experiences to connect theory with practice. Internships ideally are integrative experiences encouraging students to be active in their own learning. Experiences such as internships become "the basis for students to develop abstractions reflectively based on familiar content" (Mentkowski and Associates, 2000, p. 230). Employers commonly cite internships as the best way for students to gain practical experience and prepare them for the workplace (Oblinger and Verville, 1998).

A variety of experiential learning opportunities are sponsored by colleges and universities. The focus in this section is on internships, however, because they are often viewed as the capstone learning experience that ideally draws on previous knowledge and skills that students gain from the entire professional preparation program.

Internships are structured and supervised professional experiences in an approved organization or agency where students earn academic credit upon completion of the experience (Inkster and Ross, 1995). An internship is also sometimes referred to as *a practicum.* Although cooperative education typically involves work experiences where students are paid, internships are usually not paid. Undergraduates are supervised by personnel in the college or university and in the workplace.

High-quality internships are envisioned to follow or adhere to the seven principles of good practice espoused by Chickering and Gamson (1991). They encourage contact between faculty and students as well as develop cooperation among students. Students are exposed to numerous active learning techniques and receive prompt, ongoing feedback about their performance. Students spend specific allocated times on their multiple tasks as they strive to achieve high expectations. Finally, internships help students learn to respect diverse talents and ways of learning.

Examining Internships Through the McDonough Center for Leadership and Business, Marietta College

Marietta College offers a minor or certificate in leadership studies as a supplement to academic majors. This minor requires the completion of twenty credit hours of course work, 100 hours of community service, and a senior internship (Schwartz and Lucas, 1998). The certificate requires fifteen credit hours and fifty hours of community service. Students begin the course work in their freshman year, and the capstone experience is the internship.

Students who participate in these educational experiences are expected to achieve the skills and values that prepare them for leadership in their homes, communities, and workplaces. They are also expected to understand ethical leadership and be motivated to solve problems that face them and strengthen their group skills. Undergraduates ideally learn to view problems from various perspectives—community and multicultural as well as their own individual perceptions.

Juniors prepare themselves for the senior internship by completing an internship preparation seminar that focuses on developing specific skills. Students learn about the Career Center and its resources, but then they "move quickly to exercises intended to develop self-awareness and self-expression" (Schwartz and Lucas, 1998, p. 123). The skill assessments help undergraduates learn and communicate their own personal traits and aspirations to potential employers. Students also participate in exercises designed to improve their interviewing skills. In the second part of the seminar, students learn participant observation skills. Undergraduates are required to write critical reaction papers about the organizations in which they are involved, having observed these entities through the lens of course materials of the first four seminars on leadership (Schwartz and Lucas, 1998). Students are expected to use theories and models that they have studied and determine how they apply to issues in the workplace or organization.

All students participate in an internship during their senior year. Students assess themselves by analyzing "their ability to use an array of group skills, work with others to solve real problems, perceive and respond appropriately to different cultures, operate from a personal working definition of leadership, and form an understanding of the needs of a pluralistic democracy" (Schwartz and Lucas, 1998, p. 124). During the internship, students write their observations in a journal and use these reflections in another course that occurs after the internship is completed. In this postinternship seminar, undergraduates discuss and analyze their internships in the context of leadership topics. Plans are under way to conduct a longitudinal study of graduates.

Assessing Student Learning Through Internships at the University of Wisconsin–Oshkosh

Education faculty at the University of Wisconsin–Oshkosh reevaluated how they assessed their majors who participated in real-world experiences such as internships. To address the longitudinal, contextual, and collaborative nature of assessment, the faculty decided to use the portfolio method (Scanlon and Ford, 1998). Initially, faculty negotiated with their students about the specific outcomes that were important. Examples of outcomes included "an increased ability to plan lessons, apply ideas gained from class in practical settings, and [build] their own professional levels of confidence, competence, and comfort in the role of teacher" (Scanlon and Ford, 1998, p. 101). Faculty discussed with students what types of evidence would be collected and used to demonstrate growth and change toward these outcomes. Students are encouraged to understand that samples of their work might be the best sources of evidence to demonstrate their abilities to apply ideas and concepts explored in previous course work.

Students worked with faculty to generate criteria for judging the evidence and successful completion of stated outcomes. These criteria were broad to capture a variety of ways to document student learning, but they provided a specific framework that could be used by professors, teacher mentors, and university students in the assessment process (Ford, Anderson, Bruneau, and Scanlon, 1996). These criteria included assessments of (1) quantity of items, (2) level of creativity, (3) level of reflection, (4) appropriateness of evidence, (5) usefulness of ideas to future teaching and learning contexts, (6) self-initiated section, (7) quality of change, (8) variety of activities and evidence, (9) organization, and (10) time and effort invested. Throughout the semester, students decided which evidence to include in their portfolios that documents their learning. They were also asked to reflect on their samples of work, "what context it comes from, why it is important enough to be included in the portfolio, how it indicates growth and change, and how it shows connections between their work experience and class content" (Scanlon and Ford, 1998). Students typically discussed how their perceptions had changed as a result of their work experience, what they were learning on the job, and what challenges they were facing.

To grade the portfolios, faculty experimented with three different strategies. The initial method was to invite students to self-evaluate and grade their own work according to negotiated criteria. The professor reviewed those decisions and discussed the outcomes with each student to reach an agreement about the final grade (Ford, 1996). In a more directive fashion, an alternative strategy was to have the instructor retain full control of the assessment process by making a decision alone about what grade to assign based on criteria established by the faculty. Finally, professors also tried to read and grade portfolios according to the ratings judged by two different faculty members, who later met with the student to determine a final grade for the portfolio.

Building Communities of Inquiry and Support Through Internships at the University of New Hampshire

Since 1974, the University of New Hampshire has maintained a five-year educational program designed to teach students how to make thoughtful, effective classroom decisions (Oja, Diller, Corcoran, and Andrew, 1992). Three major components in the curriculum are designed to help their teachers become reflective decision makers. These learning experiences include course work in philosophical inquiry, the internship, and the collaborative supervisory team at the internship site. Across these experiences, students ideally gain professional knowledge that they apply to study issues as well as explore a range of alternative perspectives and options. Students examine issues in several areas of inquiry: "theories of development and learning and teaching, teaching models leading to the development of an educational philosophy and effective personal style of teaching, structure of public education and procedures for effecting change in that structure, and significant assumptions and philosophical points of view that underlie teaching and schooling and that help define a personal philosophy of education" (Oja, Diller, Corcoran, and Andrew, 1992, p. 7). Course work, in the philosophical inquiry series, consists of a cycle with four phases. In the *acquaintance* phase, students learn about a range of theories and ideally gain an understanding of other perspectives. In the *analysis* stage, students question their own assumptions and learn how to investigate different perspectives. In the *appraisal* phase, students use more rigorous methods of evaluation and systematic criteria to begin to assess their own positions. And in the *synthesis* phase, students begin to build their own philosophy of education and ideally use it to make informed, reflective decisions.

Faculty have structured an increasing emphasis on building collaborative groups for change and a vehicle for support and inquiry throughout the course work and internship experiences. In recent years, these groups have expanded to communities for faculty and school teachers as well as college students.

All students participate in a year-long internship as part of the program requirements. This internship is considered to be the centerpiece of the curriculum, as it offers students the opportunity to integrate their teaching methods with actual classroom experience. During the internship, students are viewed as *coexplorers* who are responsible for evaluating and making decisions about how to improve their teaching. The cooperating teacher and supervisor ideally assume roles as coequals.

Students also participate in two-hour internship seminars that meet each week. Students are expected to complete writing assignments each week that include letters, journals, and observation notes. Students' performance is assessed through these methods. Supervisors also gain information from their observations of students' performance in the classroom. These observations give supervisors insights into problems that students encounter. Finally, supervisory teams have been created in certain schools where several interns are placed. These teams meet regularly to identify common goals and to examine collaborative inquiry strategies. Action research projects have enabled the supervisory teams to study selected issues or problems in more depth.

Designing Strong Internship Experiences

The National Society for Experiential Education discusses key strategies for creating strong internships (Inkster and Ross, 1995). This resource provides in-depth guidance about the importance of certain steps that should be addressed. The overview of these steps discussed in this section focuses primarily on the assessment of these types of experiences.

Typically, faculty and staff identify sites for internships that are expected to promote learning. Professional development for interns is enhanced when they gain exposure to workplace problems and analyze solutions to address key issues. The selected examples in this section illustrate students as active participants who investigate real-world problems. Students' observations of others or just "job shadowing" individuals does not enhance student learning to its fullest extent.

Schön (1987) asserts that the epistemological assumptions that faculty bring to the design of an internship can dramatically affect what this experience is envisioned to accomplish and the methods by which it seeks to achieve those goals. On the surface, the major elements of internships at different colleges and universities seem to be very similar. However, Schön (1987) describes the dynamics of an internship influenced by an objectivist perspective where professional knowledge consists of facts, rules, and procedures applied uniformly to problems. The internship is a form of technical training. The instructor is primarily concerned with communicating and demonstrating that interns can apply rules and facts appropriate for professional practice. Supervisors observe students' performance, seeking primarily to point out errors in application and telling students the correct responses.

Although most internships focus on some aspects related to the achievement of techniques and skills associated with a particular professional practice, the internship can also address students' intellectual development. Thus, internships can help students learn how to reflect in action, develop new methods of reasoning, construct and test new categories of understanding, experiment with different action strategies, and try new ways of framing problems (Schön, 1987). Faculty who adopt these constructivist perspectives act as coaches who help interns become engaged with and draw on multiple ways of knowing, which advances students toward integrative knowledge. Applying routine aspects of professional practice is important, but increasingly students can encounter new situations and ambiguous circumstances that require adjustments and new solutions. Given current dynamic environments, students who are lifelong learners ideally will be able to reflect closely on their actions and be skilled in knowing what actions are most appropriate to address very complex problems.

Ideally, faculty work closely with students to identify and articulate appropriate educational objectives that focus on what students intend to learn and do in the internship. These objectives reinforce the goals of the overall internship program. Duly (1982) suggests this step is critical so that students and supervisors understand how the skills and knowledge can be demonstrated as end products of the experience and the conditions that are likely to help promote these types of skills. Ideally, learning experiences and reporting procedures should be designed to ensure that students achieve the expected learning outcomes (Duly, 1982). If students understand the learning objectives, then they can consciously work at developing them and can report their progress through reflections about the results of their efforts.

Recruiting, selecting, and placing students in appropriate internships is another important task. Students also need to be prepared for their learning and working experiences. Throughout the internship, students are supported in their learning and receive feedback through assessments and evaluations. Ideally, these assessments demonstrate the learning that students have achieved. Finally, the learning is formally reported.

Assessing the Internship Experience and Student Learning

Assessing students' work becomes challenging when undergraduates are involved in diverse professional settings that provide a variety of valuable professional experiences. Assessments of student learning in internships should provide an accurate and understandable description of learning, and the methods and reporting strategies used should enhance learning (Guskey, 1994).

One of the primary goals of the internship is to help students become more self-directed in their own learning. Therefore, the plan for assessment should provide substantial initiative for the intern to self-assess rather than ask the student to assume a passive role in being assessed (Inkster and Ross, 1995). Some programs ask interns to complete written statements at the beginning of their internships that outline job responsibilities and the goals they have set for themselves (Palomba and Banta, 1999). Other faculty ask students to write regularly in journals, describing their experiences over time. Some interns submit weekly reports documenting their specific activities or accomplishments. Undergraduates sometimes develop critical incident logs to document in detail significant or critical events when they occur. Students are encouraged to reflect on key issues and raise questions about the particular incident, to discuss their perceptions of, feelings toward, and reactions to the experience, and to analyze the incident and its implications (Inkster and Ross, 1995).

Most interns complete final reports that summarize their overall experience and critique their own performance. Interns reflect on which learning outcomes they have fully achieved and how those outcomes were reached. In addition, they reflect on areas of the internship that could be stronger or improved. In their reports, interns can discuss what activities they engaged in most frequently, the courses that best prepared them for their experiences, and whether these experiences had an effect on their career interests (Palomba and Banta, 1999).

Portfolios are another strategy to assess interns' development and progress. Interns place in the portfolio a collection of materials that they have created through the internship as well as other evidence of their performance. Materials might include evaluations written by colleagues or the supervisor as well as the intern's work—proposals, brochures, reports, workshop outlines, memos, or letters.

Group conferences and seminars on campus for students during the internship can help them continue to reach their goals (Inkster and Ross, 1995). Faculty can structure the seminars to be supportive environments where students can reflect on their experiences, interpret various elements, critically analyze problems or issues, and solve problems together. Through these group meetings, students learn about issues in other organizational contexts as well. These seminars can be a good way to gauge how much learning is occurring for the students and point out particular problems.

The on-site supervisor's assessment of the intern is also critical. Most internship programs ask supervisors to evaluate the quality of work. "Asking open-ended questions about the strengths and weaknesses of the intern's performance, specific areas where interns could improve his or her performance, and recommendations for improvements in the academic program based on the intern's performance" can be gathered from on-site supervisors (Palomba and Banta, 1999, p. 227). Most supervisors will also be asked to comment and rate specific dimensions of the intern's performance, including their ability to work independently, explore and analyze problems, communicate effectively, and generate solutions to key issues or problems.

The academic internship coordinator also assesses the progress of interns. They usually collect materials from both the supervisors and the interns. The internship coordinator typically visits each intern in the workplace several times to observe his or her performance. Often, the internship coordinator has the final responsibility for formally assessing the intern's performance and assigning letter grades or a pass-fail rating.

Summary

Information to assess the intern's performance should be collected in a variety of ways and from a variety of sources. Patterns of student performance representing their professional development will emerge as this information is fully reviewed and analyzed (Wiggins, 1993). Assessments of students in professional settings such as internships should be longitudinal, contextual, and collaborative (Sorenson, 1992). Professional growth and development occur over time as students engage in numerous learning experiences. Within the internship, it is useful to view assessment as a longitudinal process where information about the intern's performance is collected throughout the semester or year that they participate. Over time, the intern's skills and confidence in working with specific individuals in these settings should increase.

The situation in which the student works also informs the assessment. Work samples that can be collected as artifacts for assessment in the internship should always be considered with the professional context in mind (Scanlon and Ford, 1998). The context will influence the intern's efforts and products. Finally, strong internship experiences draw on assessments that are collaborative in nature. The students, on-site internship supervisors, and college or university supervisors should all be involved in the assessment. Their assessments can provide students with meaningful information so that they know their strengths and areas needing improvements. In addition, when faculty review patterns of student learning over time, they can find information that can be used to target specific changes in professional preparation programs.

Building Conditions That Promote Change

THE TYPES of major curriculum transformations discussed in this book are not easy to accomplish and take considerable time to develop and implement. To foster and sustain these curriculum reforms over time, certain conditions in the college or university culture are necessary to facilitate or support the longevity of these innovations. Serious attention to several important aspects can help lay a foundation to promote an openness to consider new ideas. Successful administrators or faculty leaders who want major reforms must first build a supportive environment that provides certain conditions on campus that are essential to bring about change.

> **Successful administrators or faculty leaders who want major reforms must first build a supportive environment.**

Creating Trust

First, a condition of trust is an important prerequisite for creating a positive attitude and openness to consider change on a college campus (Farmer, 1999a, 1999b). Administrators and faculty should work together as partners. Free and open communication among appropriate stakeholders (including students) is critical for building trust (Farmer, 1999a, 1999b). An initial focus on the potential benefits of desired change is important. This discussion includes the components of the curriculum and areas of student learning that faculty believe should be strengthened. Faculty need to understand how changes can constructively and positively influence students in professional programs to reach higher standards and be better prepared for their new roles. Faculty also may find it useful to examine models at other institutions to explore the potential aspects that can be adopted or tailored for implementation at their own university. Faculty who learn about new ideas by critiquing models at other colleges may find by talking with their peers that certain features are transferable to their own setting.

Promoting Change by a Committed Leadership

A committed and consistent leadership is a second important condition (Ewell, 1997). It is the responsibility of the top leadership and administrators to encourage innovation and to make it clear that it fully supports change agents (Farmer, 1999a, 1999b). For example, academic deans and department chairs must provide public and consistent support for curriculum reform and establish an expectation that change will occur. The committed leadership team becomes guides or facilitators of change rather than authorities who tell their colleagues what specific changes should occur. This team also provides organized coordination for the reform process. Regular working meetings with faculty are important to promote open discussions about the plans. In addition, change agents help participating professors reach a consensus about many dimensions of these new learning experiences, including learning outcomes, content, assignments, and assessment methods.

If the individuals who will most likely be affected by potential change are widely involved in the process, then their commitment will help ensure the success of the reform.

Effective planning for the creation and implementation of major curriculum reforms emphasizes a participatory process as an important means for generating support for change (Civian and Associates, 1997; Farmer, 1999a, 1999b). Organizational change always centers on people, so it is critical that leaders pay serious attention to feelings, perceptions, and symbols (Ewell, 1997). If the individuals who will most likely be affected by potential change are widely involved in the process, then their commitment will help ensure the success of the reform. Faculty should be able to participate fully in the initial stages of development or creation and implementation as well as assessment. Faculty will feel real ownership for the initiative and thus be more motivated to adopt changes. In addition, change agents should be continually open to feedback and respond to criticisms throughout the entire change process. Faculty resistance to change can be diminished if planning and implementation are open to revisions as warranted by experience over time. Finally, support for change should be sustained even after it is fully implemented. Major curriculum reforms are a continuous process that should be reexamined and updated regularly.

Designing Incremental Change

If change is introduced quickly and expected to affect the whole system simultaneously, then the likelihood is increased that the innovation may not be sustained. Although change agents may have a vision for major changes across the curriculum, it is often important to pilot test the desired innovations to discover what is working and what can be improved. Pilot projects allow faculty to experiment with these new innovations without fear of penalty if the initiative has specific problems or does not work as well as expected. This approach also provides an opportunity for demonstrating the feasibility of intended actions before moving to broad change (Farmer, 1999a, 1999b).

Large changes can be broken into smaller units that can occur sequentially over time. For example, when a college decides to implement problem-based learning, change agents can work with faculty to select a sample of courses to incorporate these reforms during the initial year. Then in subsequent years, additional faculty and classes can be added to the initiative. Such a process can help diminish resistance, because the early adopters of these initiatives can serve as mentors or role models for other faculty who contemplate changes in subsequent years. Overall, professors view incremental changes as less threatening than larger, global changes across the curriculum implemented at one time.

Some faculty are very receptive to change and adopt it faster than others. Some professors are slow to change. Rogers (1995) has consistently found that faculty accept and adopt change at different rates. The common rate of change or acceptance pattern typically mirrors a normal distribution. Approximately 2.5 percent of the faculty will be innovators, another 13.5 percent early acceptors or adopters. These professors are most likely to embrace change. About 65 percent of faculty are the majority and 16 percent are the latecomers.

Change agents can analyze their faculty groups according to the rate of acceptance for change and assign priorities and allocate resources most effectively (Middendorf, 2000). Innovators and early acceptors are open to change and will experiment with new ideas. Latecomers are a difficult group to reach despite the investment of resources to work with them. By examining innovators and early acceptors more carefully, however, change agents can identify opinion leaders and acceptable innovators, two subgroups who can influence the willingness of the majority to accept change (Middendorf, 2000).

Opinion leaders are important individuals within the early acceptors (Rogers, 1995). Although they have no official position of power, they do have considerable influence over others' attitudes and behaviors. These faculty can provide a vital network to facilitate change. They may be viewed as making careful judgments and good decisions as they observe the work of the innovators to identify strengths and then observe latecomers to learn about an idea's limitations (Middendorf, 2000). Once the opinion leaders are identified, it is critical to involve them in planning and implementing the new or revised curriculum. They may make presentations to their colleagues and discuss the new ideas with others. Opinion leaders also are important sources of information, because they fully understand and know the needs of their peers. Their reactions and responses to change can help identify the information that is needed to provide to others as well as the main concerns that should be addressed (Middendorf, 2000).

Acceptable innovators are the first individuals to embrace and make changes. They are willing to take risks, communicate with other innovators, and have information sources beyond their own immediate colleagues (Middendorf, 2000). They are most effective as pilot testers, because they are willing to experiment with new approaches that others may be reluctant to attempt. If other colleagues are interested in the change, then innovators can serve as demonstrators of the new approach and can collaboratively work with other faculty who want to adopt the change.

Educating Faculty

The preparation and education of faculty to consider and plan these changes is essential. "Faculty commitments and capabilities make or break the implementation of curriculum change, and they are central to sustaining program vitality" (Association of American Colleges, 1994, p. 44). Faculty need learning opportunities to explore new ideas and build their confidence to implement new types of curriculum change. In addition, they need to gain the necessary knowledge and expertise to experiment with new learning approaches and assessment strategies.

For some faculty, getting students to work together in groups is a new experience. Other faculty want to learn more about active learning strategies that help students become more engaged with their own development. Professional development activities are important to help faculty learn new instructional approaches such as small-group activities, case analyses, written assignments, oral presentations, and the use of technology to evaluate and use information effectively. Diverse approaches can be applied in courses that effectively promote learning outcomes.

In successful curriculum reform, change agents have thoughtfully planned and developed a series of ongoing faculty development activities. These initiatives are designed to help faculty conceptualize their new ideas and to receive constructive feedback from their peers regarding suggestions for improvement. For example, faculty who have decided to adopt problem-based learning in their courses often encounter difficulties defining open-ended, real-world problems with numerous alternatives. In a strong faculty development program, faculty leaders work with instructors to help them create these real-world problems and then continually give meaningful feedback to faculty. Faculty understand the importance of building strong open-ended problems and make informed changes based on the feedback they receive.

Some faculty development programs for new initiatives begin during an intensive one- or two-week period during the summer. Change agents find that the summer is a good time for faculty to conceptualize their changes with sufficient time to reflect on their own plans. Other faculty development activities include workshops, retreats, collaborative course development, and ongoing faculty seminars. Drawing on the problem-based learning example, faculty often need help articulating their new expectations for student learning as well as strategies for forming and evaluating group work. Many of these concepts are new for faculty, which is why a strong development program is necessary to build learning experiences over time. Most doctoral programs emphasize research tools and technical skills, leaving many new graduates "to develop their teaching skills through on-the-job training without formal attention to the literature of higher education or to the knowledge about teaching that literature contains" (Needles and Powers, 1990, p. 264).

Even though faculty may design strong plans in the summer, they need feedback during the academic year as they implement their plans. For example, faculty may have difficulties getting their student groups to work together effectively during the semester. A strong faculty development plan should include ongoing discussion mechanisms where change agents can discover the particular challenges that faculty are encountering and then provide timely feedback that gives specific strategies to address the challenges.

Professors at the University of Delaware have created a faculty development initiative for their problem-based learning initiative. Watson and Groh (2001) outline a weeklong summer institute, including the integrated curriculum that is offered to faculty—an introduction to PBL, writing effective problems, working with group dynamics, using the Web to build course resources for specific learning experiences, and assessing student learning. Faculty who have attended the previous institutes and gained substantial experience become mentors and facilitators for the current one. The result at the University of Delaware is that entire academic programs have been transformed into more active learner-centered and inquiry-based experiences. In addition, there are renewed interests and commitments to undergraduate teaching and learning in the context of this research university (Watson and Groh, 2001).

Faculty often learn best from examining each other's ideas and providing thoughtful feedback for improvement. If a campus lacks someone with substantial experience, it may be necessary to bring in an outside consultant to work with faculty on specific topics. Faculty want to be fully prepared for these changes. Administrators who assign a high priority to relevant faculty development measures demonstrate clearly their support for innovation (Farmer, 1999a, 1999b). Depending on the specific initiative, group training in information literacy, critical thinking, writing across the curriculum, or active learning strategies may be necessary for faculty who are implementing changes specifically focused on certain outcomes.

Designing Meaningful Incentives

Change agents should consider providing real incentives to gain faculty support and motivation for frequently time-consuming innovations. The key is identifying what faculty value that might be used as incentives—summer salary to work on the initiatives, release time from teaching a course during the academic year to reallocate time to implement the innovation, new support from a graduate or teaching assistant, or resources to attend national conferences.

Equally important is examining how a faculty member's participation in the innovation will be considered in promotion and tenure decisions (Civian and Associates, 1997). Participating faculty will invest considerable time as they reform their curriculum. Typically, university, college, and department evaluation criteria determine advancements in rank as well as promotion and tenure. In many colleges and universities, the focus is on research and publications. Untenured faculty may find the cost of participation too high. Successful long-term reforms will require faculty leaders to work with their peers to get curriculum development and teaching activities recognized, valued, and rewarded, particularly through promotion and tenure.

Some curriculum innovations portrayed in this book were initially funded by a grant. Internal instructional grants help support or foster innovations that faculty design but could not be implemented without additional resources. External grants from organizations such as the Fund for the Improvement of Postsecondary Education or from other professional associations (such as the American Accounting Association and the Accounting Education Change Commission) can provide important seed money to begin pilot projects designed to prepare stronger professionals for the workplace.

The major challenge is that these types of new innovations require substantial amounts of time to develop and implement, particularly as they are tried for the first time. Change agents should find ways to give faculty the necessary time to create, implement, and assess their new innovations. Real resources should be adequate and predictable so that faculty know support is available to design and implement all phases of the initiative.

Implications for the Implementation and Maintenance of Curriculum Transformations

A LTHOUGH SOME PROFESSORS HAVE SUCCESSFULLY implemented and assessed major curriculum reforms, other faculty who
are considering such major revisions may need help in reconceptualizing the
entire academic program and how individual courses contribute to or reinforce the changes. The majority of examples in this book emphasize the collaborative nature of change that results in a collegial approach to improving
the quality of student learning and thus preparing professionals to become
more effective in the workplace. Such a reform process emphasizes that serious initiatives require a systematic approach across the curriculum rather than
selective interventions by an individual faculty member for a single course.
Isolated changes are less likely to have a major impact on student learning.

Despite the desire for curriculum transformations, there are challenges to
achieving such major changes. Stark and Lowther (1988) note that "faculty
and administrators seem hesitant to invest the concerted effort needed to pursue truly substantive curricular change" (p. 15). Part of this difficulty stems
from a perceived lack of incentives for faculty to work with their colleagues,
particularly faculty in other fields. Some administrators have sought to avoid
confrontations among faculty with different perspectives by focusing on gov-
ernance issues rather than the educational program (Stark and Lowther, 1988).
Professors are also very concerned with issues of turf and resource protection,
which inhibits dialogue (Stark and Lowther, 1988). With scarce resources and
increasing competition, individual faculty members may try to document their
indispensability by attempting to take more territory through their specialized
expertise.

Almost a decade later, Ewell (1997) observed that for the most part, curriculum changes have been implemented piecemeal, both within and across institutions. In addition, they have been implemented "without a deep understanding of what collegiate learning really means and the specific circumstances that are likely to promote it" (p. 3). However, the selected examples highlighted in this book represent major curriculum transformations where groups of faculty made significant changes across their professional preparation programs that are consistent with what is known about promoting learning. These transformations also follow strong practices that can potentially lead to a high-quality curriculum that may have a more lasting impact on undergraduates.

Stating Clear and Measurable Outcomes Linked Across Courses, the Professional Preparation Program, and Institutional Levels

Across the initiatives profiled in this book, faculty clearly identified the specific learning outcomes that they wanted students to master in individual courses. These outcomes were linked to their larger professional preparation program goals and often tied to goals for general education or the core curriculum. Such learning outcomes were frequently shaped by the needs of the workplace and suggestions from employers or advisory boards. These professors, very early in the transformation process, worked to define what professional knowledge, skills, and attitudes the educated professional graduate should achieve.

Clear statements about intended learning outcomes provide the foundation for assessment at the course, program, and institutional levels. These statements also provide direction for all instructional activity and inform students about the intentions of faculty (Huba and Freed, 2000).

In these professional preparation programs, faculty created learning outcomes that were student focused rather than instructor focused. Professors articulated what students should know and be able to do rather than stating what they plan to teach. In addition, they addressed the learning resulting from the assignments or activities rather than describing only the activity itself. By consulting with external stakeholders (such as professional associations, businesses, practicing professionals, and advisory boards), faculty focused on student outcomes that were deemed important aspects of learning credible to the larger public and the workplace. Finally, faculty focused on some dimensions of learning that could be developed and assessed as the changes were implemented rather than waiting until the new curriculum had been in place for several years.

Faculty can be challenged to articulate and define outcomes, especially those that focus on writing, speech communications, teamwork, critical thinking, and information literacy. In addition, developing a range of cognitive outcomes from a basic understanding of material to advanced skills in analyzing and evaluating multiple sources of information is a new experience for faculty who have focused mainly on knowledge comprehension. Resources are available to help faculty define these outcomes.

A series of goals (Jones, 1997) in speech communications, listening, writing, problem solving, critical thinking, and critical reading can be useful to help faculty identify their priorities. Each goal inventory is based on a comprehensive review of the literature and outlines a comprehensive framework for each major skill and then defines in greater specificity key dimensions associated with strong mastery. In addition, the Association of College and Research Libraries (2000, ACRL) articulates key outcomes for information literacy. Many of these skills are interrelated, which becomes evident as one examines ACRL's definition of information literacy that includes the need for students to be able to "evaluate information and its sources critically and incorporate selected information into his or her knowledge base and value system" (p. 3). Students draw on their critical thinking skills as they search for relevant information and then critique it. In addition, "the information literate student, individually or as a member of a group, uses information effectively to accomplish a specific purpose" (p. 3). Students draw on their communication skills to work productively in teams.

Some faculty use formal strategies to reach a consensus about the most important outcomes and levels of performance (Jones, 2001), including the use of the Delphi approach, in which groups of faculty make judgments about the importance of skills through an iterative series of surveys, with the ultimate goal to reach a consensus. *Developing a Curriculum* is another technique that can be used with a panel of experts who analyze the skills, knowledge, and attitudes necessary for certain types of professional positions.

An analysis of course syllabi can determine whether learning outcomes are explicit and how they reinforce larger program goals. Program-level learning outcomes for students should be directly linked with outcomes embedded in individual courses. Often faculty actually list their program-level outcomes and then proceed to identify the specific courses designed to achieve these outcomes. Each course then consists of a series of specific learning outcomes that directly align with the program-level outcomes.

If the analysis of course syllabi reveals gaps, then faculty know the areas that they should target across their courses. In addition, they can identify important affective outcomes, including dispositions such as being open-minded, patient, or flexible that can be integrated in the curriculum. Certain psychomotor skills may be important, requiring dexterity in operating medical equipment, for example. A clear articulation of outcomes will directly address what undergraduates should know, understand, and be able to do with their knowledge and sophisticated abilities that they develop.

Designing Learning Experiences to Achieve the Selected Outcomes

Faculty identified which learning experiences would be redesigned to specifically advance the intended learning outcomes. Again, these changes were systemwide within a professional preparation program rather than minor revisions in one course or sections of a course. Making important decisions about how to build stages in skill development (over time) for students is also an important part of curriculum development (Huba and Freed, 2000).

Faculty consciously planned that certain outcomes would be reinforced across their programs. In this way, students had multiple opportunities to apply and use their skills in different and new contexts. This attribute is consistent with calls for reform by the Education Commission of the States (1995), which asserted a quality curriculum requires ongoing practice of learned skills. In addition, faculty set high expectations that moved beyond memorizing or recalling information. They wanted students to develop stronger problem-solving or critical thinking skills that required students to work with open-ended problems or issues. Such outcomes, integrated across the curriculum, can promote coherence in student learning as undergraduates draw on and synthesize their skills.

Across these learning experiences, students were actively engaged and often worked in teams as they examined complex, real-world problems. Such problems often had multiple solutions, with students having to identify the best option and justify their decisions or recommendations. These major curriculum reforms are consistent with research that finds learning occurs best in the context of a compelling "presenting problem" (Ewell, 1997). Students were also given multiple opportunities to reflect on their own learning, particularly in internships where they could critique their own performance and analyze strengths as well as areas needing improvement. They received frequent feedback about their performance, which helped them to identify ways to make constructive changes.

Selecting Multiple Assessment Methods

Another crucial dimension is the selection of multiple assessment methods that will measure the intended learning outcomes. When faculty implement major curriculum changes, it is difficult to know whether they are making a difference if there are no systematic assessments of student learning. Strongly developed assessment methods in the classroom and at the program level are important, because they help faculty to focus on improving student learning rather than reporting quantitative scores on standardized tests as the main measure of students' success.

Faculty leaders can design an ongoing, committed assessment of student learning experiences in the reformed curriculum. Such an assessment focuses on both outcomes or products and the learning process by using multiple methods.

Some assessments give students the opportunity to construct meaning and apply their skills as well as use their new knowledge. In addition, certain assessments have moved from focusing on discrete, isolated skills to integrated and cross-disciplinary assessments. Increasingly, these assessments are also moving away from a focus only on the individual student and his or her work to assessments of group collaborative products as well as group process skills. The curriculum reform and its implementation are open to modification as warranted by the findings from assessments.

Methods should include a sample of both direct and indirect assessments of student learning (Palomba and Banta, 1999). In the major curriculum transformations highlighted in this book, faculty tended to use more direct assessments of student performance that included projects, products, papers, portfolios, and exhibitions. Such assessments ask students to demonstrate what they know and can do with their knowledge. Students typically draw on their disciplinary knowledge as well as certain skills such as teamwork, writing, oral communication, or reasoning. These types of authentic assessments require students to make connections between the abilities and skills they have developed in the core or general education curriculum and the discipline-based knowledge and skills they have acquired in their majors (Huba and Freed, 2000). Such approaches break the traditional notions that writing will be taught only in English courses and that oral communications will be taught only in the required speech communications course. The focus on integrating skills with knowledge does not replace the importance of content. Students who have greater command of knowledge in disciplines can reason and communicate more effectively than undergraduates with less knowledge (Resnick and Resnick, 1992). The key is that these new approaches help students to better use and apply their knowledge in different contexts.

> **The key is that these new approaches help students to better use and apply their knowledge in different contexts.**

Students are expected to demonstrate their achievement of the learning outcomes through these assessment methods. At the program level, course-embedded assessments can provide meaningful data that can be used to determine the achievement of learning outcomes. The model at King's College used in the accounting program is an example of faculty who use course-embedded assessments to determine whether students are reaching their intended outcomes for individual courses as well as for the professional preparation program.

Indirect assessments of student learning may include surveys or interviews with students about their own experiences and self-reports about their satisfaction with their academic programs. In addition, students' perceptions about their learning and development can be useful. Assessing undergraduates during their program and then as alumni who enter the workplace can provide longitudinal data about the relevancy of their education and applications as well as preparation for their new roles.

Faculty may be overwhelmed with deciding which particular instruments are best to assess their learning outcomes as they consider designing their own method or using a commercially developed assessment measure. Recent work by Erwin (2000) reviews the wide array of instruments available to assess critical thinking, problem solving, and writing. Each instrument is evaluated for its purpose, cost, types of scores (total and/or subscores), reliability, and validity. A second sourcebook by Jones and RiCharde (in press) examines instruments that are available to assess oral communication, interpersonal skills, leadership, information literacy, quantitative reasoning, and computational skills. Faculty who are interested in getting examination copies will find specific information about the publishers so that they can determine whether selected instruments will meet their needs.

Reviewing Assessment Results to Make Targeted Improvements

Once the evidence about student performance is fully analyzed, then faculty discuss and share the assessment results, using the information to make concrete enhancements in the curriculum to strengthen student learning. Within courses, these discussions take place between individual faculty and their students, with the focus on using the results to improve student performance (Huba and Freed, 2000). At the program level, discussions occur among the entire faculty. Through a formal review of the results, professors can gain insights into the levels of learning that are being addressed and achieved in their academic programs. The assessment results may raise questions about the design of the curriculum or about the learning strategies used (Walvoord, Bardes, and Denton, 1998). Armed with this information, groups of faculty can then make informed decisions about the types of changes needed in professional education programs. They know the strengths of the program as well as the limitations, weaknesses, or gaps that are not addressed. An open environment where faculty share the assessment results with numerous stakeholder groups (including students, other colleagues, and employers) can create dialogues about what meaningful changes can be made to improve student learning.

Developing New Partnerships

Across many of the curriculum reforms highlighted in this report, faculty developed new partnerships with colleagues across the university. Often faculty in their specific professional education programs wanted to focus on certain outcome areas such as speech communications or information literacy. They believed that formal collaborations with experts in these areas on campus would be vital to creating strong learning experiences. Faculty can find valuable partners by working with colleagues in speech communications, writing, education, or library science. In this way, subject experts can develop meaningful learning experiences that directly address important outcomes by working with their colleagues in other colleges or departments. For example, the business faculty may partner with several speech communications faculty to develop a business communication course as well as integrate communications across the entire business curriculum. In many of these curriculum reforms, essential skills were embedded across the curriculum rather than addressed by only a single course.

Faculty are also forming more partnerships with schools, businesses, and corporations as they seek to expand their internship programs by providing undergraduates with more real-world experiences that often occur over longer periods of time. These external groups are also becoming more involved in formally assessing the quality of students' work, not only projects or products but also their process skills such as communications, working in groups, and problem solving. In some cases, employers can be invited into the classroom to directly observe students' demonstrations or performances. They can then be asked to assess students in conjunction with faculty members.

Undergraduates often find they get meaningful feedback from multiple assessors that can lead to improvements.

Sustaining Learner-Centered Curriculum Reforms

Clearly, faculty in some professional preparation programs are changing their entire academic curricula. These professors have developed learner-centered plans and then implemented major curriculum reforms that address their intentions. Across the examples highlighted in this report, it is clear that certain characteristics demonstrate a strong focus on the learner:

• Undergraduates are actively involved and receive ongoing feedback;
• Undergraduates apply knowledge to long-standing and new real-world open-ended issues and problems;
• Undergraduates integrate discipline-based knowledge with their process skills, including problem solving, information literacy, communications, and teamwork;
• Undergraduates understand the high expectations for learning and work;
• Undergraduates become increasingly more advanced in their abilities and skills;
• Professors guide and facilitate both individual and group work while integrating teaching and assessing across the course; and
• Professors make adjustments or revisions based on their assessment results.

Faculty are using more authentic assessments that require students to make strong connections between the abilities and skills they have learned in general education and the discipline-based knowledge and skills they have mastered in their major. Faculty are moving beyond just asking students to give the right answer to asking:

• Can students demonstrate the qualities that we value in educated persons, the qualities we expect of college graduates?
• Can they gather and evaluate new information, think critically, reason effectively, and solve problems?

- Can they work respectfully and effectively with others?
- Can they communicate clearly, drawing upon evidence to provide a basis for argumentation or justification for their position?
- Do they have self-regulating qualities such as persistence and time management that will help them reach long-term goals?
- Do they make informed decisions and judgments based upon diverse sources of information across disciplines as needed? [Huba and Freed, 2000, pp. 41–42]

Faculty who dramatically transform their curricula seek to build stronger learning experiences for their students. The Wingspread Group on Higher Education (1993) issued a major call for reform by "putting student learning first." The curriculum transformations discussed in this book demonstrate that some groups of faculty did define what students need to succeed in their programs and attempted to tailor their learning experiences to meet students' needs. They also wanted students to reach higher levels of learning and designed their curricula in an attempt to reach these intentions.

The curriculum reforms highlighted in this report demonstrate that groups of faculty can work effectively together to seriously overhaul undergraduates' learning experiences. These changes address many of the concerns expressed by employers, alumni, and policymakers. Ongoing systematic assessments of students while they are in college and then as they enter the workplace are important to target future curriculum revisions.

The challenge now is to encourage more program faculty to consider changes and find productive ways to transform their own professional preparation programs to produce stronger learners who are fully prepared for their new professional roles upon graduation. Although the work may seem daunting, we can learn from the experiences of our colleagues who have been successful in developing, implementing, and evaluating major curriculum reforms.

References

Adams, S. J., Lea, R. B., and Harston, M. E. (1999). Implementation of a serial-case pedagogy in the introductory managerial accounting course. *Issues in Accounting Education, 14*(4), 641–656.

Ainsworth, P. L., and Plumlee, D. R. (1993). Restructuring the accounting curriculum content sequence: The KSU experience. *Issues in Accounting Education, 8*(1), 112–127.

Albrecht, W. S., and Associates. (1994). An accounting curriculum for the next century. *Issues in Accounting Education, 9*(2), 401–425.

Albrecht, W. S., and Sack, R. J. (2000). *Accounting education: Charting the course through a perilous future.* Sarasota, FL: American Accounting Association.

Alverno College. (1996). *Ability-based learning program: Teacher education.* Milwaukee, WI: Alverno College.

Applegate, J., and Shaklee, B. (1992). Stimulating reflection while learning to teach: The ATTEP at Kent State University. In L. Valli (Ed.), *Reflective teacher education: Cases and critiques* (pp. 65–81). Albany: State University of New York.

Association of American Colleges. (1994). *Strong foundations: Twelve principles for effective general education programs.* Washington, DC: Association of American Colleges.

Association of College and Research Libraries. (2000). *Information Literacy Competency Standards for Higher Education.* Chicago: Association of College and Research Libraries.

Barr, R. B., and Tagg, J. (1995). From teaching to learning: A new paradigm for undergraduate education. *Change, 27*(6), 13–25.

Bedford, N. (1986, Spring). Future accounting education: Preparing for the expanding profession. *Issues in Accounting Education,* 169–195.

Bellack, J. P., and O'Neil, E. H. (2000). Recreating nursing practice for a new century: Recommendations and implications of The Pew Health Professions Commission's final report. *Nursing and Health Care Perspectives, 21*(1), 14–21.

Big Eight Accounting Firms. (1989). *Perspectives on education: Capabilities for success in the accounting profession.* New York: Big Eight Accounting Firms.

Bloom, B. S. (1956). *Taxonomy of education objectives. Handbook 1: The cognitive domain.* New York: McKay.

Boyett, J. H., and Snyder, D. P. (1998). Twenty-first century workplace trends. *On the Horizon: The Strategic Planning Resource for Education Professionals, 6*(2), 1, 4–9.

Breivik, P. S., and Gee, E. G. (1989). *Information literacy: Revolution in the library.* New York: Macmillan.

Business–Higher Education Forum. (1995). *Higher education and work readiness: The view from the corporation.* Washington, DC: Business–Higher Education Forum and the American Council on Education.

Business–Higher Education Forum. (1997). *Spanning the chasm: Corporate and academic cooperation to improve work-force preparation.* Washington, DC: Business–Higher Education Forum and the American Council on Education.

Cannon, C. A. (1998). Path charting: A process and product for linking pathophysiological concepts. *Journal of Nursing Education, 37*(6), 257–259.

Cannon, C. A., and Schell, K. A. (2001). Problem-based learning: Preparing nurses for practice. In B. J. Duch, S. E. Groh, and D. E. Allen (Eds.), *The power of problem-based learning* (pp. 165–177). Sterling, VA: Stylus.

Carnevale, A. P. (2000). *Community colleges and career qualifications.* Washington, DC: American Association of Community Colleges.

Carnevale, A. P., Gainer, L. J., and Meltzer, A. S. (1990). *Workplace basics: The essential skills employers want.* San Francisco: Jossey-Bass.

Catanach, A. H., Croll, D. B., and Grinaker, R. L. (2000). Teaching intermediate financial accounting. *Issues in Accounting Education, 15*(4), 583–604.

Cavanaugh, J. C. (2001). Make it so: Administrative support for problem-based learning. In B. J. Duch, E. S. Groh, and D. E. Allen (Eds.), *The power of problem-based learning.* Sterling, VA: Stylus.

Chickering, A. W., and Gamson, Z. F. (1991). *Applying the seven principles for good practice in undergraduate education.* New Directions for Teaching and Learning, no. 47. San Francisco: Jossey-Bass.

Civian, J. T., and Associates. (1997). Implementing change. In J. G. Gaff and J. L. Ratcliff (Eds.), *Handbook of the undergraduate curriculum: A comprehensive guide to purposes, structures, practices, and change* (pp. 647–660). San Francisco: Jossey-Bass.

College Placement Council. (1994). *Developing the global workforce: Institute for colleges and corporations.* Bethlehem, PA: College Placement Council.

Commission on Admission to Graduate Management Education. (1990). *Leadership for a changing world.* Los Angeles: Graduate Management Admission Council.

Commission on Workforce Quality and Labor Market Efficiency. (1989). *Investing in people: A strategy to address America's workforce crisis.* Washington, DC: U.S. Department of Labor.

Cromwell, L. (1993). Active learning in the classroom: Putting theory into practice. *Experiential Learning Quarterly, 18*(3), 1, 18–23.

Darling-Hammond, L. (1997). *Doing what matters most: Investing in quality teaching.* New York: National Commission on Teaching and America's Future.

Darling-Hammond, L. (1999). Educating the academy's greatest failure or its most important future? *Academe, 85*(1), 26–33.

Darling-Hammond, L., and Snyder, J. (1998). Authentic assessment of teaching in context. In *Contextual teaching and learning: Preparing teachers to enhance student success in and beyond school* (pp. 253–294). Washington, DC: American Association of Colleges for Teacher Education and Center on Education and Training for Employment, The Ohio State University.

Duch, B. J., Groh, S. E., and Allen, D. E. (2001). *The power of problem-based learning.* Sterling, VA: Stylus.

Duly, J. S. (1982). *Learning outcomes: The measurement and evaluation of experiential learning.* PANEL Resource Paper, no. 6. Raleigh, NC: National Society for Internships and Experiential Education.

Education Commission of the States. (1995). *Making quality count in undergraduate education.* Denver: Education Commission of the States.

Education Commission of the States. (1996, April). What research says about improving undergraduate education. *AAHE Bulletin,* 5–8.

Edwards, N. T. (1997). Integrating content and pedagogy: A cultural journey. *Action in Teacher Education, 19*(2), 44–54.

Eichelberger, L. W., and Hewlett, P. O. (1999). Competency model 101: The process of developing core competencies. *Nursing Health Care Perspectives, 20*(1), 204–208.

Erwin, T. D. (2000). *The NPEC sourcebook on assessment: Volume 1. Definitions and assessment methods for critical thinking, problem solving, and writing.* Washington, DC: National Postsecondary Education Cooperative and the National Center for Education Statistics.

Ewell, P. T. (1997). Organizing for learning. *AAHE Bulletin, 50*(1), 3–6.

Farmer, D. W. (1988). *Enhancing student learning: Emphasizing essential competencies in academic programs.* Wilkes-Barre, PA: King's College Press.

Farmer, D. W. (1999a). Course-embedded assessment: A catalyst for realizing the paradigm shift from teaching to learning. *Journal of Staff, Program and Organizational Development, 16*(4), 199–211.

Farmer, D. W. (1999b). Institutional improvement and motivated faculty: A case study. In M. Theall, (Ed.), *Motivation from within: Approaches for encouraging faculty and students to excel.* New Directions for Teaching and Learning, no. 78. San Francisco: Jossey-Bass.

Fink, I. (1997). Adapting facilities for new technologies and learners. In M. Peterson and Associates (Eds.), *Planning and managing for a changing environment.* San Francisco: Jossey-Bass.

Ford, M. P. (1996). Begin with the end in sight: Student negotiated evaluation in a preservice literacy education course. *New Era in Education Journal, 77*(1), 2–8.

Ford, M. P., Anderson, R., Bruneau, B., and Scanlon, P. (1996). Student portfolios in four literacy education contexts: Challenging decisions about evaluation and grading. In D. Leu, C. Kinzer, and K. Hinchman (Eds.), *Literacies for the 21st century: Research and practice. Forty-fifth yearbook of the national reading conference.* Chicago: National Reading Conference.

Gardner, P. (1998). Are college seniors prepared to work? In J. N. Gardner and G. Van der Veer (Eds.), *The senior year experience: Facilitating integration, reflection, closure, and transition.* San Francisco: Jossey-Bass.

Gardner, P., and Motschenbacher, G. (1993). *More alike than different: Early work experiences of co-op and non co-op engineers.* East Lansing: Collegiate Employment Research Institute, Michigan State University.

Grantz, R., and Thanos, M. (1996). Internships: Academic learning outcomes. *NSEE Quarterly, 21*(1), 10–27.

Graves, J., and Corcoran, S. (1989). The study of nursing informatics. *Image, 21*(4), 227–231.

Guskey, T. (1994). Making the grade: What benefits students? *Educational Leadership, 52*(2), 14–20.

Hoberman, S. (1994). Recommendations. In S. Hoberman and S. Mailick (Eds.), *Professional education in the United States: Experiential learning, issues, and prospects* (pp. 183–189). Westport, CT: Praeger.

Holton, E. F., III. (1992, Spring). Teaching going-to-work skills: A missing component in career development. *Journal of Career Planning and Employment,* 46–51.

Holton, E. F., III. (1998). Preparing students for life beyond the classroom. In J. N. Gardner and G. Van der Veer (Eds.), *The senior year experience: Facilitating integration, reflection, closure, and transition* (pp. 95–115). San Francisco: Jossey-Bass.

Huba, M. E., and Freed, J. E. (2000). *Learner-centered assessment on college campuses: Shifting the focus from teaching to learning.* Boston: Allyn & Bacon.

Hutchings, P., and Wutzdorff, A. (Eds.) (1988). *Knowing and doing: Learning through experience.* New Directions for Teaching and Learning, no. 35. San Francisco: Jossey-Bass.

Inkster, R. P., and Ross, R. G. (1995). *The internship as partnership: A handbook for campus-based coordinators and advisors.* Raleigh, NC: The National Society for Experiential Education.

Jacobs, P., and Associates. (1997). An approach to defining and operationalizing critical thinking. *Journal of Nursing Education, 36*(1), 19–22.

Jones, E. A. (1996). National and state-level policies affecting learning expectations. In E. A. Jones (Ed.), *Preparing competent college graduates: New and higher expectations for student learning* (pp. 7–18). New Directions for Higher Education, no. 4. San Francisco: Jossey-Bass.

Jones, E. A. (1997). *Goals inventories: Writing, critical thinking, problem-solving, speech communications, listening, and critical reading.* University Park, PA: National Center on Postsecondary Teaching, Learning, and Assessment.

Jones, E. A. (2001). Working with faculty to transform undergraduate curricula. In R. A. Voorhees (Ed.), *Measuring what matters: Competency-based learning models in higher education.* New Directions for Institutional Research, no. 110. San Francisco: Jossey-Bass.

Jones, E. A., and RiCharde, S. (forthcoming). *Student outcomes sourcebook on assessment: Methods for communication, leadership, information literacy, quantitative reasoning, and quantitative skills.* Washington, D.C.: National Postsecondary Education Cooperative and the National Center on Education Statistics.

King's College. (1999). *King's College 1999–2000 catalogue.* Wilkes-Barre, PA: King's College Press.

Louis, M. R. (1980). Surprise and sense making: What newcomers experience in entering unfamiliar organizational settings. *Administrative Science Quarterly, 25,* 226–251.

Luttrell, M. F., and Associates. (1999). Competency outcomes for learning and performance assessment. *Nursing and Health Care Perspectives, 20*(3), 134–141.

Manz, C. C., and Sims, H. P. (1993). *Business without bosses: How self-managing teams are building high-performing companies.* New York: Wiley.

Marshall, R. (2000). New skills for an information economy. In S. A. Rosenfeld (Ed.), *Learning.now: Skills for an information economy* (pp. 37–52). Washington, DC: American Association of Community Colleges.

Mentkowski, M., and Associates. (2000). *Learning that lasts: Integrating learning, development, and performance in college and beyond.* San Francisco: Jossey-Bass.

Middendorf, J. K. (2000). Finding key faculty to influence change. *To Improve the Academy, 18,* 83–93.

Miles, C. (1994). *The mindful worker: Learning and working in the 21st century.* Clearwater, FL: H&H Publishing.

Muffo, J. A., and Metz, N. (1996). Preparing faculty for writing across the curriculum. In T. Banta, J. P. Lund, K. E. Black, and F. W. Oblander (Eds.), *Assessment in practice: Putting principles to work on college campuses* (pp. 315–317). San Francisco: Jossey-Bass.

National Association of Colleges and Universities (1995, November). Special report: Job outlook '96. Bethlehem, PA: National Association of Colleges and Universities.

Needles, B. E., Jr., and Powers, M. (1990). A comparative study of models for accounting education. *Issues in Accounting Education, 5*(2), 250–267.

Oblinger, D. G., and Verville, A. L. (1998). *What business wants from higher education.* Phoenix: Oryx Press.

Oja, S. N., Diller, A., Corcoran, E., and Andrew, M. D. (1992). Communities of inquiry, communities of support: The five year teacher education program at the University of New Hampshire. In L. Valli (Ed.), *Reflective teacher education: Cases and critiques* (pp. 3–23). Albany: State University of New York Press.

Page, N., Geck, S., and Wiseman, R. L. (1999). College/university coordinators' perceptions of quality indicators for co-op/internship sites. *Journal of Cooperative Education, 34*(1), 43–53.

Palomba, C. A., and Banta, T. W. (1999). *Assessment essentials: Planning, implementing, and improving assessment in higher education.* San Francisco: Jossey-Bass.

Paranto, S. R., and Champagne, L. M. (1996). *Perceptions of the business community regarding program effectiveness at a selected university.* (ED 395 551)

Peterson, M. W., and Dill, D. (1997). Understanding the competitive environment of the postsecondary knowledge industry. In M. Peterson and Associates (Eds.), *Planning and management for a changing environment.* San Francisco: Jossey-Bass.

Pew Health Professions Commission. (1998). *Recreating health professional practice for a new century.* San Francisco: Pew Health Professions Commission.

Poirrier, G. P. (1997). *Writing-to-learn: Curricular strategies for nursing and other disciplines.* New York: National League of Nursing Press.

Rao, M., and Sylvester, S. (2000). Business and education in transition: Why new partnerships are essential to student success in the new economy. *AAHE Bulletin, 52*(8), 11–13.

Raymond, M. A., and McNabb, D. E. (1993). Preparing graduates for the workforce: The role of business education. *Journal of Education for Business, 68*(4), 202–207.

Resnick, L., and Resnick, D. (1992). Assessing the thinking curriculum: New tools for educational reform. In B. R. Gifford and M. C. O'Connor (Eds.), *Changing Assessments: Alternative Views of Aptitude, Achievement, and Instruction* (pp. 37–75). Boston: Kluwer.

Rogers, E. M. (1995). *Diffusion of innovations* (4th ed.). New York: Free Press.

Romanowski, M. H., and Oldenski, T. E. (1998). Challenging the status quo of teacher education programs. *The Clearing House, 72*(2), 111–114.

Ross, D., and Bondy, E. (1996). The continuing reform of a university teacher education program: A case study. In K. Zeichner, S. Melnick, and M. L. Gomez (Eds.), *Currents of reform in preservice teacher education* (pp. 62–79). New York: Teacher's College, Columbia University.

Ross, D. D., Johnson, M., and Smith, W. (1992). Developing a PROfessional TEACHer at the University of Florida. In L. Valli (Ed.), *Reflective teacher education: Cases and critiques* (pp. 24–39). Albany: State University of New York Press.

Scanlon, P. A., and Ford, M. P. (1998). Grading student performance in real-world settings. In R. S. Anderson and B. W. Speck (Eds.), *Changing the way we grade student performance: Classroom assessment and the new learning paradigm* (pp. 97–105). New Directions for Teaching and Learning, no. 74. San Francisco: Jossey-Bass.

Schön, D. A. (1987). *Educating the reflective practitioner: Toward a new design for teaching and learning in the professions.* San Francisco: Jossey-Bass.

Schwartz, S. W., and Lucas, N. (1998). Leadership education in the senior experience. In J. N. Gardner and Associates (Eds.), *The senior year experience: Facilitating integration, reflection, closure, and transition* (pp. 116–132). San Francisco: Jossey-Bass.

Smith, B. L. (1998). Curricular structures for cumulative learning. In J. N. Gardner and G. Van der Veer (Eds.), *The senior year experience: Facilitating integration, reflection, closure, and transition* (pp. 81–94). San Francisco: Jossey-Bass.

Sorenson, N. (1992). Making evaluation longitudinal: Evaluation as history writing. In K. Goodman (Ed.), *The whole language catalog supplement on authentic assessment.* Santa Rosa, CA: Macmillan–McGraw Hill.

Stark, J. S., and Lowther, M. A. (1988). *Strengthening the ties that bind: Integrating liberal and professional study.* Report of the Professional Preparation Network. Ann Arbor: University of Michigan.

Stark, J. S., Lowther, M. A., and Hagerty, B.M.K. (1986). *Responsive professional education: Balancing outcomes and opportunities.* ASHE-ERIC Higher Education Report, no. 3. Washington, DC: Association for the Study of Higher Education.

Stone, D. N., and Shelley, M. K. (1997). Educating for accountancy expertise: A field study. *Journal of Accounting Research, 35,* 35–61.

Tom, A. R. (1997). *Re-designing teacher education.* Albany: State University of New York Press.

Travis, L., and Brennan, P. F. (1998). Information science for the future: An innovative nursing informatics curriculum. *Journal of Nursing Education, 37*(4), 162–168.

Useem, M. (1995). Corporate restructuring and liberal learning. *Liberal Education, 81*(1), 18–23.

Van Horn, C. E. (1995). *Enhancing the connection between higher education and the workplace: A survey of employers.* Denver: State Higher Education Executive Officers and the Education Commission of the States.

Verhey, M. P. (1999). Information literacy in an undergraduate nursing curriculum: Development, implementation, and evaluation. *Journal of Nursing Education, 38*(6), 252–259.

Videbeck, S. L. (1997a). Critical thinking: A model. *Journal of Nursing Education, 36*(1), 23–28.

Videbeck, S. L. (1997b). Critical thinking: Prevailing practice in baccalaureate schools of nursing. *Journal of Nursing Education, 36*(1), 5–10.

Walker, R. D., and Muffo, J. A. (1996). Alumni involvement in civil engineering. In T. Banta, J. P. Lund, K. E. Black, and F. W. Oblander (Eds.), *Assessment in practice: Putting principles to work on college campuses.* San Francisco: Jossey-Bass.

Walvoord, B. E., Bardes, B., and Denton, J. (1998). Closing the feedback loop in classroom-based assessment. *Assessment Update, 10*(5), 1–2, 10–11.

Watson, G. H., and Groh, S. E. (2001). Faculty mentoring faculty: The institute for transforming undergraduate education. In B. J. Duch, S. E. Groh, and D. E. Allen (Eds.), *The power of problem-based learning.* Sterling, VA: Stylus.

Wiggins, G. (1993). Assessment: Authenticity, context, and validity. *Phi Delta Kappan, 75*(3), 200–214.

Wingspread Group on Higher Education (1993). *An American imperative: Higher expectations for higher education.* Racine, WI: The Johnson Foundation.

Name Index

A
Adams, S. J., 34
Ainsworth, P. L., 32, 33
Albrecht, W. S., 20, 21, 27, 29, 30, 31
Allen, D. E., 41
Anderson, R., 69
Andrew, M. D., 70
Applegate, J., 50, 59, 60, 61

B
Banta, T. W., 73, 74, 90
Bardes, B., 91
Barr, R. B., 17
Bedford, N., 21
Bellack, J. P., 35, 36
Bloom, B. S., 33
Bondy, E., 57, 58
Boyett, J. H., 2
Breivik, P. S., 43
Brennan, P. F., 43, 48, 49
Bruneau, B., 69

C
Cannon, C. A., 35, 36, 42, 43
Carnevale, A. P., 1, 6, 8, 12
Catanach, A. H., 31
Cavanaugh, J. C., 42
Champagne, L. M., 9
Chickering, A. W., 67
Civian, J. T., 78, 83
Corcoran, E., 70
Corcoran, S., 48

Croll, D. B., 31
Cromwell, L., 66

D
Darling-Hammond, L., 50, 51, 52, 53, 54, 56
Denton, J., 91
Dill, D., 3, 4
Diller, A., 70
Duch, B. J., 41
Duly, J. S., 73

E
Edwards, N. T., 57
Eichelberger, L. W., 38
Erwin, T. D., 91
Ewell, P. T., 78, 86, 89

F
Farmer, D. W., 24, 27, 77, 78, 79, 83
Fink, I., 4
Ford, M. P., 69, 70, 75
Freed, J. E., 17, 18, 86, 88, 90, 91, 94

G
Gainer, L. J., 6, 8, 12
Gamson, Z. F., 67
Gardner, P., 9, 10, 23
Geck, S., 66
Gee, E. G., 43
Grantz, R., 66
Graves, J., 48

Subject Index

Measure of Epistemological Reflection, 60
Medical Scholars program, 41
Michigan State University, 53
Michigan State University study (1998), 9–10
Minority workforce population, 4
Mississippi Council of Deans and Directors of Schools of Nursing, 38
Missouri Western State College, 56–57

N

National Association of Colleges and Employers, 8
National Commission on Teacher and America's Future, 51, 52
National Society for Experiential Education, 71
National Teachers Exam, 57
Nursing program reforms
    Case Western Reserve University, 48–49
    defining important student outcomes and, 36–38
    responses to, 35–36
    San Francisco State University, 43–45, 46t–48
    summary of, 49–50
    University of Delaware, 41–43
    University of Memphis, 38–41

O

Opinion leaders, 80

P

PBL (problem-based learning) [University of Delaware], 41–43
Pew Health Professions Commission, 36
Portfolio (internship), 74
Professional education
    defining/ideal outcomes of, 5–7
    examining criticisms/reforms of, 7–14
    purpose/scope of report on, 14–15
    See also Undergraduate education
Professional education criticisms
    current student/alumni views about preparation, 9–11

employer beliefs about student preparation, 7–9
Professional education reforms
    in accounting programs, 20–25, 26t, 27–35
    in nursing programs, 35–45, 46t–50
    recommendations for, 11–14
    responses to call for, 17–20
    in teacher education programs, 50–63
    See also Change
Professional fields
    basic skills needed in, 6–7
    competencies of, 5–6, 44, 55
Project Discovery (PD) students [University of Illinois], 22, 24

S

San Francisco State University (SFSU), 43–45, 46t–48
Student learning outcomes
    assessing internships and, 69–70, 73–75
    implementing curriculum reforms for, 86–94
Student portfolios, 74
Students
    advantages of internships for, 65–67
    assessing internship experience/learning by, 73–75
    assessing learning through internships, 69–70
    building communities of inquiry/support through internships, 70–71
    designing strong internship experiences for, 71–73
    examining Marietta College internships for, 67–68
Students with disabilities, 53

T

Teacher education program reforms
    Alverno College, 54–56
    Kent State University ATTEP program, 59–61
    Missouri Western State College, 56–57
    responses to, 50–51

ASHE-ERIC
Higher Education Reports

The mission of the Educational Resources Information Center (ERIC) system is to improve American education by increasing and facilitating the use of educational research and information on practice in the activities of learning, teaching, educational decision making, and research, wherever and whenever these activities take place.

Since 1983, the ASHE-ERIC Higher Education Report series has been published in cooperation with the Association for the Study of Higher Education (ASHE). Starting in 2000, the series has been published by Jossey-Bass in conjunction with the ERIC Clearinghouse on Higher Education.

Each monograph is the definitive analysis of a tough higher education problem, based on thorough research of pertinent literature and institutional experiences. Topics are identified by a national survey. Noted practitioners and scholars are then commissioned to write the reports, with experts providing critical reviews of each manuscript before publication.

Six monographs in the series are published each year and are available on individual and subscription bases. To order, use the order form at the back of this issue.

Qualified persons interested in writing a monograph for the series are invited to submit a proposal to the National Advisory Board. As the preeminent literature review and issue analysis series in higher education, the Higher Education Reports are guaranteed wide dissemination and provide national exposure for accepted candidates. Execution of a monograph requires at least a minimal familiarity with the ERIC database, including *Resources in Education* and the current *Index to Journals in Education*. The objective of these reports is to bridge conventional wisdom and practical research.

Advisory Board

Susan Frost
Office of Institutional Planning
and Research
Emory University

Kenneth Feldman
SUNY at Stony Brook

Anna Ortiz
Michigan State University

James Fairweather
Michigan State University

Lori White
Stanford University

Esther E. Gottlieb
West Virginia University

Carol Colbeck
Pennsylvania State University

Jeni Hart
University of Arizona

Review Panelists and Consulting Editors

Recent Titles

Back Issue/Subscription Order Form

Copy or detach and send to:
Jossey-Bass, A Wiley Company, 989 Market Street, San Francisco CA 94103-1741

Call or fax toll-free: Phone 888-378-2537 6:30AM – 3PM PST; Fax 888-481-2665

Back Issues: Please send me the following issues at $24 each
(Important: please include series abbreviation and issue number.
For example AEHE28:1)

_____

_____

_____

$ _____   Total for single issues

$ _____   SHIPPING CHARGES: SURFACE   Domestic Canadian
First Item $5.00 $6.00
Each Add'l Item $3.00 $1.50
For next-day and second-day delivery rates, call the number listed above.

Subscriptions   Please ❑ start ❑ renew my subscription to *ASHE-ERIC Higher Education Reports* for the year 2_____at the following rate:

U.S.	❑ Individual $150	❑ Institutional $150
Canada	❑ Individual $150	❑ Institutional $230
All Others	❑ Individual $198	❑ Institutional $261
Online Subscription		❑ Institutional $150

**For more information about online subscriptions visit
www.interscience.wiley.com**

$ _____   Total single issues and subscriptions (Add appropriate sales tax for your state for single issue orders. No sales tax for U.S. subscriptions. Canadian residents, add GST for subscriptions and single issues.)

❑Payment enclosed (U.S. check or money order only)
❑VISA ❑ MC ❑ AmEx ❑ Discover Card #_____ Exp. Date _____

Signature _____ Day Phone _____
❑ Bill Me (U.S. institutional orders only. Purchase order required.)

Purchase order # _____
Federal Tax ID13559302   GST 89102 8052

Name _____

Address _____

_____

Phone _____ E-mail _____

For more information about Jossey-Bass, visit our Web site at www.josseybass.com

PROMOTION CODE ND03

Elizabeth A. Jones is an associate professor in higher education leadership at West Virginia University. She has provided leadership for undergraduate program assessment across WVU and is currently the director of graduate programs in higher education leadership. She is also the senior associate editor for the *Journal of General Education.* Jones has served as the external evaluator of two large-scale problem-based learning initiatives funded by The Pew Charitable Trusts Foundation at the University of Delaware and Samford University. She is also the external evaluator for an inquiry-based curriculum transformation in the biological sciences funded by the National Science Foundation at California State University–Fullerton. Jones has served as a researcher for the National Postsecondary Education Cooperative and the Working Group on Student Competencies. She currently is creating a sourcebook with colleagues for NPEC and the Working Group on Student Outcomes. While Jones worked at Pennsylvania State University, she served as the principal investigator for a series of research studies funded by NCES that identify essential skills college graduates should master in critical thinking, problem solving, writing, speech communications and listening, and critical reading. She also directed a large-scale assessment project supported by the Fund for the Improvement of Postsecondary Education and has written about assessment and curriculum issues throughout her career. Her work has been published in *Assessment Update, New Directions for Institutional Research, New Directions for Higher Education, The Journal of General Education,* and *Innovative Higher Education.* She edited *Preparing Competent College Graduates: Setting New and Higher Expectations for Student Learning* (Jossey-Bass, 1996).